DOMESTIC DARKNESS

DOMESTIC DARKNESS

An Insider's Account of the January 6 Insurrection, and the Future of Right-Wing Extremism

JULIE FARNAM

PUBLISHING

New York, NY

Ig Publishing
Box 2547
New York, NY 10163
www.igpub.com

ISBN: 978-1-63246-160-5

"Truth will ultimately prevail where there is pains to bring it to light."

—George Washington

CONTENTS

Introduction

Three days before a violent mob attacked the seat of American democracy, Julie Farnam sat on her bed and in just a few minutes wrote five words that forecasted the bedlam on January 6, 2021: "Congress itself is the target."

The Federal Bureau of Investigation didn't say that. The Department of Homeland Security's Office of Intelligence and Analysis didn't say that. *None* of the leading federal agencies in the intelligence community put out such an admonition in writing. In fact, no one produced or disseminated *any* comprehensive intelligence bulletin whatsoever about the warnings in plain sight in the lead-up to January 6.

In the end, it was one man who ended the unblemished history of the peaceful transfer of power in this country— Donald J. Trump. To what account the former president will be held remains to be seen. That story is still being written.

But—Trump's singular blame notwithstanding—there were several weak and/or blind spots in our institutional defenses on

January 6—many of which predate even the former president's rise to political power—that merit study, scrutiny, and solving. *Domestic Darkness* attempts to do just that.

Told from the perspective of a woman seeking to amplify her voice in a male-dominated space, Farnam takes an introspective and intimate look at what went wrong inside the US Capitol Police before, during, and after January 6. Farnam spares no one from the bruising truth—not even herself—as she candidly details how she went from presciently raising the alarm on the prospect of historic violence on January 6 to striking up a romance with an officer now accused of colluding with the enemy and unwittingly being used by him to feed violent extremists insider information.

In the days before January 6, 2021, the Capitol Police were mum about their preparations—even to their colleagues in law enforcement. "We had had issues understanding, getting the full picture of US Capitol Police's operational posture and what their planning was," said Christopher Rodriguez, Director of the Homeland Security and Emergency Management Agency.[1]

Washington, DC Mayor Muriel Bowser was struck when, right before a joint press briefing on January 4, she asked the Capitol Police representative, "[W]here does your perimeter start?" According to Bowser, the man got

up out of the room, call[ed] somebody. And the next

thing I know he can't participate in the conference"[2]
She went on to say, "that should have been like a trigger
to me . . ."[3] Like these people, they don't want to answer
questions about their preparation.[4]

On January 5, 2021, Valerie Hasberry, Chief Security
Officer for the Architect of the Capitol, forwarded an alert to the
Capitol Police about an individual calling online for thousands
to "go to Washington Jan 6 and help storm the Capital [sic],"
adding that "we will storm the government buildings, kill cops,
kill security guards, kill federal employees and agents."[5]

"There is now chatter on Parler about storming the Capitol,"
Hasberry wrote at the time. "Please let me know if there are any
updates to credible threats."[6]

She received a response just fifty-eight minutes later.

"There is no talk about any credible threats or storming the
Capitol," she was told.[7]

And the rest, as they say, is history.

Ultimately, there may have been a collective myopia
in underestimating the threat from a right-wing crowd
traditionally seen as friendly to law enforcement. These were
the same people who came to the defense of police during
the social justice protests after the murder of George Floyd.
These were the same people waving thin-blue-line flags, the
same flags they would use to bruise and batter the police during
the riot. But the writing was on the literal wall—on Facebook

feeds and Twitter threads and TheDonald.win posts: Anyone standing in Trump's way was the enemy, including the boys and girls in blue.

Serving as a foil to Farnam was former Capitol Police Chief Steven Sund, who sat at the top of the chain of command on January 6. I sat across from both Farnam and Sund as lead questioner for the House Select Committee to Investigate the January 6th Attack on the US Capitol. Despite having read Farnam's bleak prognosis—"Their target for the protest is Congress[;] that in itself doesn't send up a bunch of red flags for me," Sund told the committee[8]—he nevertheless stayed the course on an operational plan that he maintained included "all the available resources I could deploy."[9] But all-hands-on-deck didn't really mean all-hands-on-deck, as preapproved officer leave was not canceled,[10] which meant that only 923 officers out of 1,840 (or 50 percent) of the force were on duty at 7:00 AM on January 6, 2021. By two o'clock—the height of the insurrection—that number had only grown to 1,214 (or 66 percent of the force). The peak number of officers on January 6 (1,457) never eclipsed 79 percent.[11] "I would have hoped it would have been higher," Sund told the committee.[12]

Sund also over-relied on bike racks as the main security measure separating throngs of lawless rioters from the halls of Congress, although Valerie Hasberry conceded they lacked the staff to man the racks.[13] In addition, bike racks work only under the assumption that the crowds on the other side are law-abiding or—as Hasberry, put it, "otherwise people can, like you said, hop over or remove it or cut it or move it out of place to enter."[14]

To this day, Sund doubles down on his claim that "this was a colossal intelligence failure,"[15] on January 6, basically pointing the finger at the division where Farnam served as second in command. But when challenged, even he had to admit that the intelligence was there, it just wasn't used. The committee asked him, "It was more we didn't somehow use, distribute, synthesize, operationalize the stuff that we did get, right? We learned, but we didn't somehow get it vetted enough that it didn't translate into sufficient planning?"[16]

"It's a fair translation," he answered.[17]

In *Domestic Darkness*, Farnam produces more than just a postmortem on the failings of the Capitol Police. She also lays out a digestible guide to the groups on the front lines of domestic terror, digging into how vulnerable people get drawn to destructive ideologies and how white supremacy is fueling a movement that federal law enforcement calls the leading threat to our country. Farnam sees in our present echoes from our past, such as the Oklahoma City bombing, Waco and Ruby Ridge.

But this is also about our future. The extremist groups that stormed the Capitol are still with us, turning from national to local politics.[18] Regrouping, recharging, "stand[ing] back and stand[ing] by" should former President Trump reclaim the most powerful post in the world and call on them to finish what he started.

Our democracy barely held on January 6, 2021. The insurrection may have been quelled, but the threat is ongoing. What we learn and what we next do about it is all that matters. *Domestic Darkness* is an important part of helping us understand the lessons of January 6, so that we can take the correct action going forward.

—**Robin M. Peguero**, author of *With Prejudice* (2022) and *One in the Chamber* (2024), was investigative counsel on the Select Committee to Investigate the January 6th Attack on the U.S. Capitol and wrote Chapter Seven, "187 Minutes of Dereliction of Duty," of the Committee's Final Report, along with appendices on January 6 intelligence and the delayed response from the DC National Guard.

PREFACE

When I realized how bad it was going to get, the first thing I thought about was my children.

Since we were still in the middle of the pandemic, my kids—a kindergartner and a first grader—were not in school, but were in a virtual learning pod with other children on Capitol Hill, a few blocks away from my office. A few blocks from the Capitol.

"I need you to get the kids now," I said to my *au pair* over the phone. "They need to get away from Capitol Hill and out of the city."

"I was just about to eat lunch, can I get them after?" my *au pair* replied.

"No! I need you to do it now."

When my au pair arrived at the learning pod, she took my daughters downstairs and out onto the sidewalk to await their ride back home. There were already several protesters

walking toward the Capitol. My *au pair* told me that some
were dressed in yellow and black—likely Proud Boys—while
others were decked out in red MAGA attire. Seeing this, she
became frightened—she was Brazilian and was familiar with
right-wing leaders, having experienced the election of Jair
Bolsonaro—and ushered the kids back into the building to wait
inside for the car. Later she called to let me know they had
made it to our home in Arlington, Virginia, sounding unsettled
by her encounter with the protesters. Her fears were not quelled
as the day went on and she saw what unfolded just a couple of
blocks away from where she had stood with my children. My
children, too, were scared.

I began working as the United States Capitol Police's (USCP)
assistant director of intelligence nine days before the 2020
presidential election. The country was, without a doubt,
contentious, divided, and hateful, a far cry from the America
I wanted my daughters to inherit. And the impending election
only seemed to deepen the chasm between people who
supported President Donald J. Trump and those who were
more than ready for Joe Biden to replace him.

Right around this time, the Department of Homeland
Security announced that the most likely terrorist threat to the
United States would come from domestic violence. It was those
on the far-right, blindly bewitched by Trump, who posed the
most serious threat to the nation. We faced an enemy from

within, and it was left to me to sort through the violent and racist social media postings, and the ramblings of Trump, in order to warn the Capitol Police of what was to come. I had to do this while also having to contend with a team that largely lacked the skills and training to make any meaningful contributions to our intelligence collection or analysis and adamantly opposed any efforts to learn or to change. It was like trying to push a boulder up a mountain.

"All of us here today do not want to see our election victory stolen by emboldened radical-left Democrats, which is what they're doing. And stolen by the fake news media. That's what they've done and what they're doing. We will never give up, we will never concede . . . And we fight. We fight like hell. And if you don't fight like hell, you're not going to have a country anymore," Donald Trump told the crowd who had gathered on January 6, 2021 to contest the certification of the presidential election by Congress. In the short time I'd been with the USCP, I had seen enough intelligence to know what kind of people made up that crowd. I knew the extremist groups they belonged to, the bizarre and far-reaching conspiracies they believed in, the hatred that drove them. And I had tried to raise the alarm, time and again, in the days leading up to January 6; warning that this moment was coming and that we weren't prepared for it.

Once I knew my children were safe, all I could think about was how heavy the wooden cabinet in my office was. My eyes scanned the rest of the room, looking at what other furniture I could move if I needed to barricade the door. For the only time in my career, I was happy to not have windows in my office. Despite the blue line flags some of the insurrectionists waived, indicating their support for the police, it was clear by the actions I was seeing with my own eyes—swinging those flags to hit officers, using the ends to stab those trying to protect the Capitol—that they actually hated law enforcement. My building, which sits about a block from the east front of the Capitol, had "Capitol Police" etched into stone on the front door, making it—and me—a target.

I planned in my head how to secure the door. The wooden cabinet wouldn't be enough to hold back a determined crowd. No, it would require the cabinet *and* my desk, because the cabinet had some height and I wouldn't want it to topple over and create an opportunity for them to storm in. I had to see my children again. That door had to be kept closed.

ONE

Change and Resistance

I did not want the job, but I desperately needed it. I had been working for the United States Citizenship and Immigration Services (USCIS) for thirteen years. During that time, I had witnessed countless naturalization ceremonies, where immigrants became proud American citizens. These rites never ceased to move me in how they embodied the hope and optimism the United States symbolized to so many people around the world. This was the heart of our country, the ideal.

Having grown up in Stoneham, Massachusetts, I knew that this idealistic vision of our nation could coexist with darker truths. First settled by colonists in 1634, Stoneham was a small town where everyone knew everyone else, and quaint red brick buildings housed small businesses like chocolate shops and the community theater. Figure skater Nancy Kerrigan was born there, and her father was said to have worked three jobs to support her burgeoning career. On the face of it, this probably sounds like a lovely slice of Americana.

However, by the time I was in high school, some of my classmates had become skinheads and white supremacists and were causing trouble in our idyllic little enclave. I remember a school dance where my friends and I dressed up in muumuus and competed in a lip-synching contest, singing along to "Age of Aquarius." We won the contest and as a prize received a seventy-five-dollar gift certificate to Newbury Comics, which I later used to buy a Pearl Jam CD.

But on the sidelines of the dance, sitting against the wall of windows that overlooked the grassy courtyard where we'd play hacky sack during lunch, were several young men, their heads shaved, watching. "We got some skinheads in the house?!" the DJ yelled. The crowd cheered. I was both fascinated and fearful. No one seemed to want to do anything about them, or the town's growing drug problem. I grew frustrated by Stoneham's failure to address its own issues. I didn't want to live in a place that seemed to breed and tolerate hate.

I left home as soon as I graduated high school, determined to make a difference in the world. I took my experiences—photographer for the school newspaper, candy striper at a local hospital, a generally good student without much effort—and dove into my studies in college. I must have been in a rush because it took me three years, instead of the typical four, to finish my undergraduate degree in sociology at Simmons College (now University) in Boston. I graduated with honors.

I then took my righteous sense of justice to law school, which I immediately hated: sitting in the law library, writing brief after brief, and then hoping I understood the legal concepts adequately enough to be able to answer the questions the professor would pepper me with during class. I was the youngest in my class, and wasn't mature enough to comprehend what one needed to do to be successful in that environment. I left after a semester, self-conscious about what felt like my very first failure.

Then came a series of jobs in Boston, where I often found myself assisting immigrants. I worked in the Office of International Affairs at Emerson College, helping the international students, some of them real princes and princesses in their home countries, maintain their visa status. I volunteered in the immigration clinic at the International Rescue Committee, aiding newly arrived refugees with their immigration paperwork. I worked at an English language school where one of the 9/11 hijackers had been enrolled, leaving after the leadership of the school refused to abide by the new immigration mandates, much to my frustration. I eventually opened my own English language school in East Boston, the first stop in America for many new immigrants. It was a challenging endeavor because many of the students, undocumented and living in poverty, lacked any formal education. Many were illiterate even in their native language. But I gained satisfaction in knowing I was helping. Ultimately, I closed the school when it became apparent that it would never be profitable.

I then went back to school and earned a master's degree in intercultural relations, eventually finding the professional home I'd dreamed of in government service. I got a job with USCIS as an immigration officer working the front counter at the Boston office. There I spent my days listening to individuals who had issues with their immigration cases. In a post-9/11 world, processing immigration cases with all the newly required security checks often caused years-long delays. Many people cried as they told me their stories. Many were angry. I had passports thrown at me, I was called a Nazi, one person blamed me for his wife's suicide. It was here that I learned to communicate clearly and how to not be frazzled when I was surrounded by chaos.

During my time at USCIS, I also served as Field Operations lead on the Boston Marathon bombing investigation. For many long days and nights after the incident, I researched Tamerlan and Dzhokhar Tsarnaev, their family, friends, and associates. I received USCIS's Heritage Award for my efforts, the second highest award the agency bestowed. After the San Bernardino terrorist attack in 2015, I led a multi-agency task force to develop recommendations on how to revamp the immigrant fiancé(e) visa process. I also managed the operational portfolio for intercountry adoptions, an area fraught with human trafficking and child abuse; I even visited a Haitian prison to further explore the issue. After the Department of Homeland Security's Office of Inspector General uncovered paper fingerprint records that had not been digitized, allowing individuals to commit fraud by assuming a new identity, I led the effort to set up a unit focused exclusively on denaturalizing the nearly 2,000 people whose criminal activity had escaped detection prior to the digitization of their fingerprint records.

After a few years in Boston, I was eager to see what it might be like to work in Washington, DC, the center of the political universe. So, I applied for an opening at USCIS's headquarters, a position monitoring the agency's Government Performance and Results Act measures. I got the position, then told my husband about it. He decided to stay behind in Massachusetts, thinking I would hate Washington and/or the job. However, I ended up loving both, so two years later, he moved down to be with me.

We bought a house in Arlington, Virginia, started a family, and then things began to unravel. We had been together for over twenty years. I had met him in high school and married young. This was what I thought was expected of me: find a man, fall in love, get married. He was painfully shy and quiet, socially awkward, and very sensible, which stood in deep contrast to me. I had dreams and lacked the staunch pragmatism he possessed. My approach to life was decidedly riskier and more rebellious. I would pave my own path and accept the rewards and consequences as they came. He had plans and dutifully executed them without surprise.

I had seen too many instances among my own relatives of women staying married to their own detriment. I resolved that that would never be me, that I would never set that sort of example for my daughters. Generations of bad marriages would end with mine. Quietly, I began saving my money and preparing to move out and start fresh with the girls. I didn't want money or alimony or retirement from my ex. I didn't want anything. I worked hard to refinance our house so that the mortgage was only in my name. But being on my own was harder than I had expected. In those first few months, independence was difficult, particularly as it pertained to finances. I had a mortgage now that was solely my responsibility, utility bills, and childcare expenses, and there was no one there to help.

An agency under the Department of Homeland Security (DHS), USCIS administers the country's immigration and naturalization system, which includes providing benefits to those in the United States as well as those seeking to come here. From green cards to naturalization to work visas, USCIS is funded not by the US government, but by the application fees it collects. Even before COVID-19, the agency was having financial issues. Once the pandemic hit, it was the figurative nail in the coffin. Seventy percent of its workforce—myself included—were given furlough notices. I had been doing immigration work for so long, I didn't know if I could succeed anywhere else.

I ended up interviewing for the intelligence director opening with the Capitol Police, only to find out I was more qualified to work there than I thought. Rising through the ranks at USCIS, I had eventually settled into intelligence, overseeing the vetting of immigration applicants for ties to terrorism, espionage, and trafficking. Prior to my departure, I had been enrolled in the DHS Senior Execute Service development program. I was the only female in my cohort. Not only did I have the necessary technical and leadership skills, but I had the tenacity and perseverance required to be a change agent.

Although Jack Donohue from the New York Police Department was ultimately hired to be director, I performed well enough in my interview to become assistant director, a position they created for me. Jack and I tentatively divided the workflow, with him being responsible for the strategy and vision of the division, and me handling the day-to-day operations and managing the team responsible for gathering intelligence. Jack enjoyed being at the center of things and meeting with members of Congress and other decision-makers. I enjoyed finding solutions to complex problems, and in joining the Capitol Police, I had my work cut out for me.

On its most basic level, intelligence often starts with a question. For example: Is this person a terrorist? Is the applicant working on behalf of a foreign government? Did this individual really murder a police officer in Iraq? Is this a threat to our national security? Many people think it takes special military training or genius to work in the field, but that's not so. You can learn it, as I did, and become good at it.

The intelligence needs of the United States Capitol Police (USCP) are a combination of what you might find in traditional law enforcement (i.e., where is the criminal activity and who is committing it?) and more overarching issues, such as who is plotting a terrorist attack and whether Russia is trying to hack our computers. On top of that, the Capitol Police deals with politics in ways that no other police department in the country does because of the 535 politicians it serves and protects. Although its 1,800 officers view themselves as street cops, they really aren't.

In its two-mile jurisdiction, the Capitol Police guard the entrances to several congressional office buildings and the grand Capitol edifice itself. They also conduct sweeps of cars along the campus's perimeter, provide protection for leadership, and control crowds during demonstrations. Compared to other police departments, the USCP make arrests infrequently, and when it does, it's usually for things like protesting where one shouldn't be, stealing plants from the Botanical Gardens, driving without a valid permit, or defacing public property.

Occasionally they deal with more serious matters, but those investigations are often turned over to the Metropolitan Police Department or FBI. In this sense, the Capitol Police are more like the Secret Service, a federal agency and a protective force rather than a law enforcement agency.

I was told in my job interview that the team I'd inherit at the USCP would need a complete overhaul. But it was only when I was given a departmental audit which had been conducted by the USCP's Office of the Inspector General in 2016 that it became clear how much work this was going to take. The audit concluded that the intelligence division did not maintain up-to-date guidance or standard operating procedures for many of its processes, among them the dissemination of information, handling of classified information, and collecting and evaluating intelligence from open sources. It appeared that none of the inspector general's recommendations had been implemented in the years since the report had been released. *The Washington Post* would later write that the division "was widely seen as an embarrassment."[1] It was cruel to say, but accurate.

With the growing number of threats made against members of Congress and the Capitol itself during the Trump administration, it was immediately clear to Jack and I that we not only needed to get our division better trained at collecting and analyzing basic intelligence, but we also needed to rebuild its reputation so that those within the Capitol Police as well as other agencies took us seriously. And we'd have to do all of it in a very short period of time. It would become one of the most extensive challenges of my career.

It did not help that the culture of the Capitol Police is not one that embraces outside perspectives. The USCP are an isolated bunch that close themselves off from other agencies whose feedback could prove valuable. While it may be similar to the Secret Service in structure and function, the USCP often actively refuses to interact with other agencies that could help it unearth and make sense of the threats it receives. When I arrived, I was told on more than one occasion that I was not allowed to share any information or documents with outside agencies because the legislative branch wasn't subject to Freedom of Information Act (FOIA) requests, and the Capitol Police didn't want any of their information or documents accidentally released by another agency. When I worked for USCIS, I had to respond to FOIA requests all the time. These requests didn't concern me because I was doing things above board. The Capitol Police shouldn't have feared FOIA requests either, and they most definitely should be subject to them. However, what may have started as a desire not to release information without its permission turned into a perverse tendency to withhold even the most mundane facts, a secrecy between the different levels within the Department, and an environment that prized silence over sharing.

I ruffled feathers almost immediately. In my first days on the job, I met individually with the analysts in our division to get a sense of what they did, what their challenges were, their professional goals, and how I could help them to reach them. Most of these meetings were conducted virtually, due to the pandemic. This put me at a disadvantage because no one could see me in person. They couldn't see my manner or my smile. All they had from me up to those first virtual meetings were emails, with no intonation, no emotion, no personality.

Change is difficult under any circumstance, but when it became clear to the people working at the intelligence division that I was about to change the way they had been doing things for several years—and in some cases, decades—many were displeased. One employee even snarled at me, saying, "YOU need to learn before you start trying to change things." But I was learning plenty after only a few days, and my main takeaway was that there were members of the team who were not doing proper intelligence work during a contentious political season, with a growing domestic extremist threat brewing.

Prior to the 2020 election, we had received a threat against a member of Congress and the president. We had a duty to warn the Secret Service, and it should have been normal protocol to send threats that did not fall under the Capitol Police's jurisdiction to the responsible agency. When I asked one of the analysts in our division to send the threat over, they resisted, saying it was a task for the Threat Assessment Section.

I realized that my team had never been empowered to take initiative and had not been taught how to do what was right. Instead, they had become dependent on others. Eventually they had come to accept that little should be expected of them, and their performance reflected that sentiment. Because I didn't want this threat to fall through the cracks, I sent it to the Secret Service's Protective Intelligence Unit myself. It would not be the last time I would need to take matters into my own hands.

Beyond the bureaucratic systems that seemed to offer my team ways to hide from doing real work, the division's focus was also misguided. For example, I reviewed the several-pages-long intelligence assessment my team wrote prior to my arrival for the presidential election on November 3, 2020. It seemed odd that the report included an addendum about the left-leaning activist group, ShutDownDC. The group had started off advocating for environmental protection policies and then began to embrace other social causes important to the left. I had concerns about profiling a group that was largely engaged in First Amendment activities and non-violent civil disobedience. On November 3, the group's plan was to watch the election returns on a Jumbotron in Black Lives Matter Plaza, some sixteen blocks west of the Capitol. To me, it seemed that the activities they had planned did not warrant the focus my team paid to them. At the time, all indications were that Trump was going to lose, which would be cause for celebration—not violence—among ShutDown DC and other similar groups.

More interesting to me was the scant mention of right-wing extremist groups in the report. As someone new to the division, and to the world of domestic terrorism (I had dealt almost exclusively with foreign terrorist organizations at USCIS), I still recognized that my team's focus was misplaced. I had heard all the rhetoric leading up to the election and knew there were conspiracy theories, claims of election fraud and people willing to fight to keep Trump in office. All of that was coming from far-right elements focused on undermining our democracy. To me, that threat should have been given more prominence. But, in the brief time we worked together, my predecessor didn't see it that way.

When I had begun my new job, I was told I would overlap for a few weeks with Norm Grahe, then the Director of Intelligence, before Jack Donohue took over. The expectation was that Grahe would show me the ropes. But by Election Day, just a week after I started, Grahe officially checked out. The morning of the election, he sent an email to the Intelligence and Interagency Coordination Division or IICD saying it was "confusing" to have two supervisors and that he was turning things over to me.[2] All future taskings would be coming from me and he would stand down. This email was sent soon after I had called him to get some basic information about how things were done at the Capitol Police and within IICD. How were taskings normally sent out? Who handled what? What were the schedules of the employees? Did we have any tracking or accounting of the work we did?

In response to my questions, he said, "You are the most anxious person I know."

"I'm not anxious, I am ambitious. There's a difference," I replied.

And then he was gone, and I was the one in charge.

The GOP's "shadow committee" report for January 6 stated that "Grahe intended to remain on the job to train [Farnam]. According to a USCP source who testified to investigators, Farham [sic] declined."[3] In truth, I tried to sit down with Grahe to have constructive conversations about the team, but he largely refused.

By the end of Election Day, my first day alone in the supervisor role, we still did not know whether Trump had been re-elected. Because many people voted by mail, sixteen states had not completed their vote counts. The *New York Times* declared "Biden Beats Trump" on its front page three days later, with Biden crossing the 270-electoral-vote threshold necessary for victory. Trump not only refused to concede but spent the next few weeks challenging the outcome in court. He was not successful, but his followers were increasingly determined to fight for him. And he was happy to fan their angry, white-hot flame.

TWO

The Gathering Storm

When Donald Trump ran against Hillary Clinton in 2016, his advisor Roger Stone prepared to fight a potential Clinton victory with a concept called Stop the Steal. Designed to claim that Trump's opponents were going to "steal" the election from him through massive voter fraud, Stone first introduced Stop the Steal during the Republican primary, before escalating it during the general election.[1] Clinton did not win, so Stone's campaign to install Trump through claims of election fraud became unnecessary.[2]

The concept came in handy, however, when Trump lost in 2020, and #stopthesteal exploded online after the election. On November 4, 2020, the day after the election, a Tea Party activist named Amy Kremer created a Facebook group with the name, which reportedly added 100 new members every ten seconds.[3] By the time Facebook removed the group from its platform the following day, saying it was "organized around the delegitimization of the election process," the page had amassed 360,000 followers. A week later, on November 13, 2020, far-right activist and Stone associate Ali Alexander incorporated Stop the Steal, using it as a vehicle to raise money.[4]

Though we didn't have a clear enough picture of it at the time, Alexander and Kremer weren't the only ones fomenting a rebellion in plain sight. Another person who was involved—someone that I would become very familiar with—was Cynthia "Cindy" Chafian,[5] then of Women for America First. Right after the election, Chafian began organizing what was being referred to as the Million MAGA March, scheduled to take place on November 14, 2020. I attended the National Park Service meetings about the event so that we could get a sense from Chafian of the logistics around the march. The meetings were held virtually. While Chafian had experience planning events, she was frequently late to our meetings, and was prone to misplacing documents and not completing tasks on time. In his interview with the House Select Committee, Robert Glover, then head of the Special Operations Division of the Metropolitan Police Department, would describe Chafian[*] as

---

[*]. According to Chafian's LinkedIn profile, she is the Executive Director of Firebrand Action and Media and Director of Coalitions and Engagement for Moms for America, both positions she began in the immediate aftermath of the insurrection. Moms for America secured a permit on Capitol grounds for January 5. Up until January 2021, Chafian listed herself as being on the board of the political

a "puppet on a string," explaining that he believed she was the front person for a larger group who were coordinating this and future MAGA rallies, including January 6.[6]

In general, the details of the meetings with Chafian were mundane: how many people would be at the rally, how many port-a-potties would be on site and where would they be located, who was going to clean up the trash. There wasn't a lot of discussion about who would be attending or speaking. But it didn't matter, as anyone had a right to demonstrate under the First Amendment. But that was at the micro level. At a macro level, this event was about to say something bigger about America and serve as a warning of the things to come.

Our intelligence assessment for that first MAGA rally was exclusively focused on the extremists who were likely to be in attendance, many of whom used direct communication methods and encrypted messaging apps that would make them difficult to monitor. We also noted that "domestic violent opportunists may attach themselves to otherwise peaceful demonstrations in order to commit acts of violence, destroy property or sow civil

---

action committee WomenUnitedPAC. The PAC was registered with the Federal Election Commission as Women United, Inc. It was founded in 2012, and at that time it was active on social media, mostly focused on Hillary Clinton and Benghazi. Chafian was listed as the treasurer of the PAC from 2013 to 2016. The PAC was terminated prior to the 2018 election cycle and did not appear to have raised any reportable amounts of money during its existence, based on its FEC filings.

unrest." Improvised melee weapons and projectiles could not be ruled out either.[7] I never received any feedback or questions about the assessment.

As expected, pro-Trump crowds gathered in Washington, DC, on November 14 to claim that the election was being stolen from the president—and them. They vowed to take back their country. The question was from whom? Was it Democrats? Progressive women? People of color? Jewish people? The LGBTQ+ community? Immigrants? Gun haters? All of the above? Whatever or whomever it was, *something* was threatening their existence and Donald J. Trump was the only person they felt could act in their best interests. Fighting to keep him in office was the only solution that made sense to them.

Not all the states had certified a winner by this point, so the marchers still believed Trump had a chance. They had many theories for why the vote count hadn't gone in favor of Trump to that point: that some election officials had failed to count votes; that voters had cast ballots using dead people's identities; the voting machines were defective; mail-in ballots had been submitted fraudulently; and that the voting systems had been hacked by China. Cindy Chafian lined up speakers who reinforced these views, including Alex Jones and Owen Shroyer of InfoWars; Mike Lindell, the MyPillow guy; Representative-elect Marjorie Taylor Greene of Georgia; and former Trump advisor Sebastian Gorka. Trump himself motored through the excited crowd, causing his Secret Service agents to run alongside the vehicle to push people back.

By evening, tensions had boiled over, leading to bloody brawls and a stabbing. Antifascist groups gathered in front of the hotels where Trump supporters were staying, while police officers stood as a defensive wall between the two sides. California-based hate and extremism researcher Brian Levin called the event the debut of the pro-Trump insurgency, which at the time should have raised more eyebrows than it did.[8] After all, insurgencies are generally armed and fast-moving affairs fought by irregular bands of people against a larger foe. The Prussian general and military theorist Carl von Clausewitz viewed these groups of fighters as "a kind of nebulous, vapoury essence."[9] Perhaps that's why it was so difficult to see where things were headed at the time. This were a scattered and disorganized threat. With limited exceptions, they were not overtly plotting to abolish democracy.

There were twenty-three arrests that day, from across the ideological divide. The march may have been over, but the thing about Clausewitz's "vapoury essences" is that they have a way of slipping through shackles, between cracks, and underneath doors to achieve their desired end. Over the next few weeks, Trump's minions would regroup and focus on Washington, DC, again, like a cloud destined to deluge the very foundation of our country.

On December 12, 2020, two days before the electoral college confirmed Joe Biden as the 46th president of the United States, there was a second Million MAGA march, with Trump's supporters continuing to protest the election results. Again, there were clashes between protesters and counter protesters. Four people were stabbed and thirty-three were arrested. The Proud Boys appeared, with some members holding up white power signs as they marched through Freedom Plaza. The group's leader, Enrique Tarrio, also went on a public tour of the White House and then posted about it on the right-wing social media app, Parler. In his post, he curiously stated that his visit "shows we've come a long way," even though the White House said that he hadn't been invited and had not met with President Trump. The next evening, the Proud Boys tore down Black Lives Matter signs at two historically Black churches in the city. The vandalism was captured on video and shared widely.

On December 14, the electoral college votes were confirmed and Joe Biden was declared the winner. "Once again in America, the rule of law, our Constitution, and the will of the people have prevailed. Our democracy—pushed, tested, threatened—proved to be true and strong," Biden declared.

But Trump still refused to concede. On Fox News, he said, "I worry about the country having an illegitimate president, that's what I worry about. A president who lost and lost badly."[10] His advisor, Stephen Miller, downplayed the importance of the electoral college vote and said that Trump would continue to fight the result until Inauguration Day.[11]

Right after the electoral college votes were confirmed, pro-Trump groups began submitting permit requests to demonstrate at the Capitol on January 6, 2021, the day a joint session of Congress would certify the votes. As a rule, permits are submitted to the Special Events Section of the Capitol Police for review, before coming to the intelligence division for an assessment. After the intelligence division completes its report, it is sent, along with the application and supporting documentation, to the Chief of Police's office, where it is typically approved. After that, anyone requesting a permit would be in constant communication with an officer who would tell the person or organization what is and isn't allowed, depending on the area where the demonstration is to take place. Due to the pandemic, event permits at that time limited the number of demonstrators around the Capitol to fifty people in a given area.

On December 15, Women for a Great America applied for a permit to pray on the Independence Avenue side of the Jefferson Building of the Library of Congress. This was the first permit request for January 6.

Four days later, President Trump erroneously tweeted that it was "statistically impossible [for him] to have lost the 2020 election." He urged his followers to come to Washington for a big protest on January 6. "Be there," he tweeted. "Will be wild!"

After that, a floodgate of permit requests opened.

On December 21, the day far right protesters stormed the Oregon statehouse demanding the state end its COVID-19 restrictions, two permit requests came in, from One Nation Under God, and from Bryan Lewis. Both intended to protest election fraud in swing states on the northeast corner of the Capitol, across the street from the Supreme Court. On December 23, Virginia Freedom Keepers submitted a permit to rally outside of the Russell Senate Office Building. That same day, I submitted an update to Sean Gallagher, the Deputy Chief of the Capitol Police, portraying a growing sense of what we might be facing. To my knowledge, that document was never distributed beyond the Capitol Police leadership.

On Christmas Eve, we got a permit request from Rock Ministries International, which wanted to hold a "prayer campaign encouraging pastors, leaders and citizens to pray for the United States" on the Independence Avenue side of the Cannon House Office Building. Finally, on December 29, Jesus Lives applied for a permit to pray on the west side of the Capitol reflecting pool. There was no escaping it: Prayer and protest would encircle the Capitol on January 6.

If all these groups followed the COVID rules then in place, we would be dealing with 300 protesters within our jurisdiction on January 6. But there were other demonstrations we'd have to consider that day, according to permit requests we were seeing for other parts of town. Women for America First would be hosting a "Save America" rally at the Ellipse, a fifty-two-acre park south of the White House, where President Trump was scheduled to speak. Although the permit was originally for 5,000 people, it was amended and approved on January 5, 2021 to allow for 30,000 participants.** The Silent Majority grabbed a spot for 250 people on the National Mall between Thirteenth and Fourteenth Streets. Cindy Chafian, acting on behalf of The Eighty Percent Coalition, landed a permit to hold the "Rally to Revival" in Freedom Plaza, some two blocks east of the Ellipse. That permit was capped at 5,000 participants, though more were expected.

I sat in on a call with the National Park Service, the Metropolitan Police Department (MPD), and others who wanted to ask Chafian about her plans. Having dealt with her already, we had well-founded suspicions about her intent. When asked about speakers for her event, her responses were nondescript, bordering on evasive. She never provided information about how she was advertising her event or how she would attract participants.

"Every time you come around, there's trouble," MPD Commander Robert Glover told Chafian.

Then came the distractions. On Christmas Day, an RV exploded

**. National Park Service Permit # 21-0278, approved January 5, 2021.

in the middle of Nashville, damaging forty-one buildings in a historic part of town[12] and causing telecommunications outages in parts of Tennessee, Kentucky, Indiana, Alabama, Illinois, Georgia and Missouri.[13] I gathered all the information I could about the incident and wrote the report myself, not wanting to bother my team on a holiday. Because it impacted critical infrastructure, there would certainly be congressional interest in what happened, which is why we needed to conduct our own review. The bombing would be followed by vandalism to the homes of Senate Minority Leader Mitch McConnell and Speaker of the House Nancy Pelosi.[14]

On December 31, I raised concerns that One Nation Under God and Bryan Lewis might be a front for Stop the Steal. While trawling through various social media sites and messaging apps, as well as Stop the Steal's own website, I'd seen chatter that various high-profile speakers with links to Ali Alexander's organization would be appearing at the same spot reserved for these two, as far as we were told, unrelated protests. And these speakers were encouraging their followers to attend. We had also seen social media with people posting pictures of their weapons and saying that they'd be coming to Washington armed, so I was concerned about how things might escalate. In an email, I told the Capitol Police leadership that:

Stop the Steal has a website www.wildprotest.com, that instructs its followers to gather in/around Area

8 on Capitol grounds on 1/6. A map included on the website shows the exact location where the protesters should gather. It also lists several speakers and many of those speakers are the same as the flyer provided to USCP by One Nation Under God, including Members of Congress. One Nation Under God . . . said they were incorporated as an organization for this event only. It's odd that a group created for this protest only and previously unknown would draw all those high-profile speakers. Bryan Lewis's protest has essentially the same purpose as the One Nation Under God protest . . . In our meeting with the Eighty Percent Coalition this morning, the organizer indicated that Ali Alexander, head of Stop the Steal, will be speaking at a protest at the Capitol on 1/6.[15]

I began to suspect that Stop the Steal wanted to surround the Capitol with permitted events. Areas 8 and 9, which are along First Street across from the Supreme Court, were prime locations. Thomas Caldwell, a member of the Oath Keepers, posted online that "it begins for real Jan 5 and 6 . . . when we mobilize in the streets. Let them try to certify some crud on Capitol Hill with a million or more patriots in the streets. This kettle is set to boil."[16]

Ultimately, the Capitol Police approved the permits, in spite of the concerns I raised.

The Capitol Police prepared for January 6 as if it were any other protest. In their view, there was no need to call out the National Guard for any reason other than to help with traffic. There was no public acknowledgment from them that a known far-right, democracy-denying group—Stop the Steal—was planning a large scale rally on Capitol grounds.

By this time, Trump had exhausted his legal challenges to the outcome of the election and had become convinced that what was normally a ceremonial electoral college vote certification could be overturned by his own vice president, thus keeping him in office, perhaps forever. "Mike Pence didn't have the courage to do what should have been done to protect our Country and our Constitution . . . USA demands the truth!" Trump tweeted. Once he was so convinced, it didn't take much for him to convince his followers, too.

As we got closer to January 6, and more intelligence came in, it was clear that we needed to provide another update. Initial efforts were not promising. One analyst found twenty-eight Facebook pages with people saying they were going to Washington on January 6. The "We The People" Facebook page had one person going and five people interested. The "Southern MD Stop the Steal MAGA March" page had ten going and twenty-four interested. On and on it went, the numbers slowly growing, and this didn't include data from Parler, Donald.win, or other fringe sites. The analyst concluded the assessment by saying, "Many of the posts are calling for peaceful protests, while a few are calling for armed participation."[17] There were only three sentences about Stop the Steal.[***]

I began to compose my own assessment, which included information from intelligence and law enforcement partners and other items I had surfaced myself. The result wasn't perfect, but it was a marked improvement from where we had begun. I sent the assessment to Chief Gallagher. He agreed that things were looking bad, and that we needed to stress that in our overall analysis. I rewrote the analysis, and on January 3, 2021, it took me about three minutes to type out the inescapable conclusion I had reached after reviewing all the intelligence I had at my disposal:

> Supporters of the current president see January 6, 2021 as the last opportunity to overturn the results of the presidential election. This sense of desperation and disappointment may lead to more of an incentive to become violent. Unlike previous post-election

---

[***]. These are the three sentences: "The statement also says they are 'working closely with StopTheSteal.com.'" "On the StopTheSteal. com webpage, an event is listed for January 5, 2021, between 1400–1700 hrs at SCOTUS. The event is sponsored by Virginia Women for Trump."

protests, the targets of the pro-Trump supporters are not necessarily the counter-protesters as they were previously, but rather Congress itself is the target on the 6th. As outlined above, there has been a worrisome call for protesters to come to these events armed and there is the possibility that protesters may be inclined to become violent. Further, unlike the events on November 14, 2020, and December 12, 2020, there are several more protests scheduled for January 6, 2021, and the majority of them will be on Capitol grounds. The two protests expected to be the largest of the day—the Women for America First protest at the Ellipse and the Stop the Steal protest in Areas 8 and 9—may draw thousands of participants and both have been promoted by President Trump himself. The Stop the Steal protest in particular does not have a permit, but several high-profile speakers, including Members of Congress, are expected to speak at the event. This combined with Stop the Steal's propensity to attract white supremacists, militia members, and others who actively promote violence, may lead to a significantly dangerous situation for law enforcement and the general public alike.

Gallagher shared my conclusions with the USCP inspectors and other leadership. In a perfect world, leadership would have shared the information with the officers further down the chain, but that didn't happen, perhaps because their lack of faith in our division was so deeply ingrained.

On January 4, 2021, I briefed the Capitol Police leadership about the January 6 demonstrations. It was a conference call, and I could tell that participation was limited. On conference calls there was a tendency to check emails and do other work while passively listening, which is what I expected was happening on this call. Once I had shared our findings, no one on the call had much to say, so we wrapped things up.

On January 5, I held a two-hour training with my team about basic open-source research methods that would come in handy during the scheduled demonstrations the next day. The team was argumentative and resistant, but it was necessary to get them up to speed, or at least try to. Some said it wasn't helpful, but had they paid attention, they would have acquired at least some basic abilities in collecting intelligence from open sources, a skill they sorely lacked.

I awakened early on the morning of January 6. I hated alarm clocks and rarely use one, instead opting to wake up naturally to start my day. But that day, unsettled with anticipation, my internal clock was set earlier than usual. Since starting this new job, I had been taken away from my kids more often than I would have liked, and that weighed on me. They wouldn't be up for another hour or so. I made myself some coffee and scrolled right-wing fringe social media sites, something I had become accustomed to doing each morning since starting at the Capitol Police. It was much of the same chatter I had been seeing for days. Though I had just awakened, I was already tired. It was going to be a bad day, I knew, despite that no one else seemed concerned.

Later that morning, we had another call updating our intelligence assessment. I was concerned that no one from the Uniformed Services Bureau was present because this was the division that includes nearly all the officers on the force. If anyone needed to know what to expect, it was them. But this was the way they had always done things, so I pressed on. I laid out my concerns about the protests, and then underscored them with five words that should have spurred the Capitol Police leadership into action: "Protesters see this as war."

I waited to see if anyone had any questions or wanted me to elaborate on what I had just said. No one said a word. After a few more moments of awkward silence, Sean Gallagher concluded the call. No one acknowledged what I had just told them, refusing to accept that a storm was headed our way.

THREE

Forces at Play

In tribute to extremist marches of the past, they came in the dark of night, carrying torches. "You will not replace us," they chanted. With anger and acrimony, they marched through the streets, fighting with counter protesters along the way. The police largely stayed out of the scuffles. That was until one of the marchers, James Alex Fields, drove his Dodge into a group of counter protesters, and then reversed the car, driving into more. Dozens of people were hurt, and one was killed, but the end result was much greater than just a physical altercation. More than any other event in recent history, the Unite the Right rally in Charlottesville, Virginia, on August 11 and 12, 2017, was responsible for the advent of mainstream hate in America.

In the press release announcing his sentencing for twenty-nine violations of the Matthew Shepard and James Byrd Jr. Hate Crimes Prevention Act, the Department of Justice noted that Fields "used social media accounts to express and promote white supremacist views; to express support for the social and racial policies of Adolf Hitler and Nazi-era Germany, including the Holocaust; and to espouse violence against African Americans, Jewish people, and members of other racial, ethnic, and religious groups he perceived to be non-white."[1] Several days after the march, President Trump famously declared that there were "some very fine people on both sides" of the rally. In doing so, Trump gave white supremacists and antisemites throughout the country a voice and a platform. In turn, they not only supported him, but also fought for him on the battlefield of January 6.

In its most extreme form, white supremacy expresses concern about a changing environment and perceived loss of control for white people, often dubbed the "great replacement." The phrase was coined by Brenton Tarrant, the individual who committed a deadly attack on a community center and mosque in Christchurch, New Zealand, in 2019. Though he gave it a name, the concept has long been employed by many on the far-right to justify their desire to promote a white, Anglo-Saxon society. Within the United States, the concept hearkens back to the nineteenth century's "racial suicide," when a predominately protestant population worried that catholic Irish immigrants would overtake the country.[2] This inherently racist idea was based in the belief that whites of western European descent were superior to other races and ethnicities, and that immigration was a threat to them.

During the Trump presidency, white supremacy made its way into the mainstream. The crossover from something that had lurked in the shadows of American culture to being on full display was readily apparent on January 6, 2021. But this change didn't happen overnight. For many years, despite so-called "dog whistle" appeals from different politicians and groups, overt racist ideology was not embraced by most Americans. To overcome that, extremist groups started disguising their beliefs as something more palatable for the general public. By targeting immigration and immigrants, and claiming they were abusing resources, increasing crime, and contributing to an overall reduction in the intelligence of the United States, the narrative shifted the focus from the frank "great replacement" discussion to one more acceptable to the masses. This is not unique to the United States. Similar trends have evolved in Brazil, Hungary, Italy, and elsewhere.[3]

This type of "white extinction" ideology was discussed extensively in the manifesto of Peyton Gendron, the person responsible for the shooting at a supermarket in Buffalo, New York, in 2022, killing ten. Most of his victims were African American and he targeted the supermarket because of the large African American population in the surrounding area. His manifesto was lengthy, running nearly 200 pages, but is more than a diatribe of extremist ideology—it is a how-to manual for future attacks.*

Gendron opens with an explanation as to why he chose to commit his terrorist attack. With no ambiguity, he asks himself the question, "Why did you decide to carry out the attack?" To which he answers: "To directly reduce immigration rates . . . To intimidate the replacers already living on our lands . . . To agitate the political enemies of my people . . . To incite violence . . . To show the effect of direct action, lighting a path forward for those that wish to follow."[4] The remainder of the manifesto provides a step-by-step outline of how to conduct a "successful" attack, including the type of equipment needed, how to choose a location and conduct surveillance, and how to use technology to maximize livestreaming, among other considerations.

Just as Gendron's manifesto was posted on social media, extremist ideology has often propagated online. One such forum for this is known as the Red Elephants, founded in 2017 by Vincent James Foxx, who goes by Vincent James. James is a Holocaust denier who promotes conspiracy theories, white nationalism, and antisemitism. He speaks openly and frequently

---

*. The manifesto written by Anders Breivik, the terrorist who killed seventy-eight people in Norway in 2011, ran over 1,500 pages and served as a source of inspiration for many extremists, including Gendron.

about the "great replacement." James was present at the January 6 insurrection.[5] His videos were prominent on YouTube, and although he was eventually banned from the platform, the videos can still be found elsewhere on the internet. Following his ban, he migrated to fringe social media platforms including Bitchute,[6] Gab,[7] and Telegram.[8] Nearly all of his social media posts feature information on how to donate to the Red Elephants. Among other things, the group actively promoted the Unite the Right rally.

Another group, VDARE, has long served as an inspiration to many white supremacists. Founded by Peter Brimelow in 1999, the group developed close ties to political pundits, including Pat Buchanan and Ann Coulter.[9] The group's name pays homage to Virginia Dare, the supposed first English—and Christian—child born in America, who later disappeared, thought to be taken by a Native American tribe. VDARE's flag, with red and blue stripes, white stars, and the image of a lion in the center, was prominently visible during the riots on January 6. Trump also used a similar logo during his 2020 presidential campaign.[10, 11, **]

Racism was not just something reflected in the Trump

**. During the Trump administration, the group received a multi-million-dollar donation from DonorsTrust, an organization that purported itself to provide charitable giving, but had funded things such as climate change denial, groups promoting Islamophobia, and other far-right ideology.

campaign's imagery. Policies implemented under his administration, such as the ban on Muslims, and the eventual ban on most immigration during the pandemic, the cruel separation of children and families and the failed attempts at building a wall at the southern border, all underpinned a racist agenda. When Trump said in June 2015, during the announcement that he was going to run for president, that, "[w]hen Mexico sends its people, they're not sending their best. They're not sending you . . . They're sending people that have lots of problems, and they're bringing those problems with us. They're bringing drugs. They're bringing crime. They're rapists,"[12] he set up a dichotomy between his presumed superiority of white Americans and the supposed inferiority of brown-skinned immigrants.

These policies have been venerated by other extremist groups, such as Patriot Front, which were also present at the Capitol on January 6. Founded by Thomas Ryan Rousseau in 2017 in Fort Worth, Texas, Patriot Front is known for its outlandish displays, with members marching wearing facemasks to disguise their identities, and holding shields painted red, white, and blue. Rousseau was also the founder of the white supremacist group, Vanguard America, which was the primary organizer of the Unite the Right rally. (The group disbanded after the rally).

Choreographed and recorded, Patriot Front's marches are uploaded onto the "Patriot Front Videos" Telegram page and other fringe social media platforms, where they serve as inspiration to other white supremacist groups as well as a recruitment tool.[13] When they aren't marching, the group hangs banners on highway overpasses, defaces signs and murals that do not support their ideals, such as those supporting LGBTQ+ or Black Lives Matter, and reprogram electronic road signs.[14] More recently, Patriot Front has engaged in humanitarian acts such as removing graffiti,[15] collecting litter,[16] and passing out meals to the homeless,[17] [18] making them even more dangerous by engaging in activities that appear legitimate. Two people associated with Patriot Front were charged in the insurrection.

Also present on January 6 was the National Socialist Club 131, or NSC-131 as it is commonly known, an influential neo-Nazi group based in New England. The numbers "131" come from the letters "ACA," an abbreviation for "Anti-Communist Action." Founded by Christopher Hood in 2019, the group has grown steadily since its creation, branching outside of New England into Florida, Kentucky, Texas, Virginia, Indiana, and Arizona.[19] On January 6, 2021, a member of the group stole the helmet of a Capitol Police officer and posted a picture of it on the group's Telegram page.

NSC-131 and others such as the Rise Above Movement are considered accelerationists: white supremacists and/or neo-Nazis who want to provoke a civil war to accelerate a complete societal collapse. Once society is destroyed, they can then rebuild it in an image that amplifies their belief in the superiority of the white race. Many white supremacists and neo-Nazis participated on January 6 because they saw it as an opportunity to accelerate the fall of the United States. They nearly succeeded in their quest.

Bridging the gap between white supremacy and anti-government sentiment is the Proud Boys. Most people know of the group because of the acknowledgment Trump gave them during the first presidential debate in 2020.

"Are you willing, tonight, to condemn white supremacists and militia groups and to say that they need to stand down and not add to the violence in a number of these cities as we saw in Kenosha and as we've seen in Portland?" the moderator, Chris Wallace, asked Trump.

"Sure, I'm willing to do that . . ." Trump responded, talking over Wallace.

"Then do it. Go ahead, sir."

"I would say, I would say, almost everything I see is from the left-wing, not from the right-wing. I'm willing to do anything. I want to see peace."

"Then do it, sir," Wallace interjected.

"Say it. Do it. Say it." Biden encouraged.

"Do you want to call them, what do you want to call them? Give me a name, give me a name, go ahead. Who would you like me to condemn? Who? The Proud Boys? Stand back and stand by . . ."[20]

And just like that, the Proud Boys became a household name in America.

The group, whose members liked to refer to themselves as "western chauvinists," was founded by a British Canadian, Gavin McInnes, a fifty-something-year-old known for pranks like implying he ate cornflakes soaked in urine and putting objects up his rear end. His juvenile attitude infused the ethos of the group, which enjoyed engaging in childish behavior, and the attention it got them.[***, 21] As an initiation into the Proud Boys, prospective members were beat up until they could name five different breakfast cereals, a tradition that allegedly started with a fart joke.[22]

McInnes grew up well-to-do, but like many other privileged boys, was never able to channel his potential into something that could positively contribute to the world. He was a co-founder of Vice Media, but left the company in 2008, and descended into a world of hate. He started the first chapter of the Proud Boys in 2016 in New York. He is also the host of the far-right online video show, *Get Off My Lawn*.[23]

Ideologically, the Proud Boys believe manhood and Western culture are being attacked. Though they are not overtly white

***. There are four levels of membership within the Proud Boys: level one is someone who will state publicly they are a member, level two has completed an initiation ritual, level three is someone who has gotten a Proud Boys tattoo, and the highest level involved those members who have fought antifa.

supremacists, they have frequently joined forces with racially motivated groups. The group's chairman from 2018 to 2021, Enrique Tarrio, is of Afro-Cuban descent, a fact that the Proud Boys were more than eager to point out to demonstrate that they were not racists. The son of Cuban immigrants, Tarrio's family fled oppression only to raise a son who promoted it. Tarrio's rise within the Proud Boys provided a convenient ideological shield for the group's effort to disguise a dogma that has increasingly promoted white racial ideals.

The group has also organized its own demonstrations, intended to be controversial and draw counter-protesters, such as their "End Domestic Terrorism" rally in Portland, Oregon, in 2019. At that rally, which drew many white supremacist and militia groups, members argued that antifa was a domestic terrorist group that needed to be stopped. The rally was organized by Tarrio and Joe Biggs,[24] both of whom would later be convicted of seditious conspiracy for their involvement in the January 6 insurrection.

Antifa and far-left groups are a frequent target and obsession of the Proud Boys and others on the far-right, including Trump. From a political perspective, it makes sense—shift the focus to the bad behavior of your adversaries. And to be clear, in the months leading up to the 2020 presidential election and the subsequent MAGA rallies, antifa did more to hurt its cause than help it. They were no better than the militias and the other domestic terrorists on the right, particularly their behavior in Portland, Oregon, which involved rioting, looting, arson, and the destruction of property.

Trump's singular focus on antifa however, and overt support of extremists on the right, as we saw in Charlottesville and with the Proud Boys—and we have seen in his post-presidency, such as his 2022 dinner with white supremacist Nick Fuentes—demonstrates a blatant disregard for other extremist groups operating in and outside of the United States. For example, on January 5, 2021, the day before the insurrection, he issued a memorandum saying that Section 212(a)(3) of the Immigration and Nationality Act extended inadmissibility to members of antifa.[25]

The Immigration and Nationality Act is the set of laws that govern U.S. immigration (i.e., who gets to come and stay in this country and for how long) and nationality (i.e., who is a citizen of the United States and who can become a citizen). The law was originally passed in 1952 and has been amended many times since. Section 212 governs who is not allowed to be admitted into the country. Trump's memorandum said generally, "Section 212(a)(3)," but the text of the memorandum was referencing more specifically Section 212(a)(3)(B), which pertains to terrorist activity, not "organized criminal activity" as the memorandum was titled. This section of law says that:

"(a) Classes of aliens ineligible for visas or admission

. . . (3) Security and related grounds (B) Terrorist activities (i) In general any alien who-(I) has engaged in a terrorist activity; (II) . . . is engaged in or is likely to engage after entry in any terrorist activity . . . (III) has, under circumstances indicating an intention to cause death or serious bodily harm, incited terrorist activity; (IV) is a representative . . . of-(aa) a terrorist organization . . . ; or (bb) a political, social, or other group that endorses or espouses terrorist activity; (V) is a member of a terrorist organization . . ."

US citizens are not subject to Section 212 of the Immigration and Nationality Act; therefore, the memorandum was addressing foreign terrorist organizations. With the memorandum, Trump was essentially declaring antifa a terrorist organization. While the definition of terrorist activity within the immigration context and what it means to have engaged in terrorist activity[26] could potentially be applicable to someone associated with antifa, it could also apply to the Proud Boys, Three Percenters, the Atomwaffen Division (now the National Socialist Order), and The Base, all of which have been designated in other countries as terrorist organizations.[27][28]

And all of whom were out in force on January 6, 2021.

FOUR

The Anti-Government

The attack on the Capitol did not come out of nowhere. It was the result of over three decades of white supremacist and militia activity that has been steadily gaining a foothold in the United States. From January 6, 2021, you can draw a direct line back a quarter of a century to the 1995 Oklahoma City bombing, and the violent episodes a few years earlier in Ruby Ridge and Waco.

In terms of numbers of people killed and injured, the April 19, 1995, Oklahoma City bombing remains the most devastating act of domestic terrorism in US history. Just as 9/11 was to foreign terrorism, the bombing of the Alfred P. Murrah Federal Building in downtown Oklahoma City prompted the government, for the first time, to start looking seriously at domestic terrorism. The bombing would also serve to inspire anti-government and militia groups for decades to come.

Timothy McVeigh, the perpetrator of the bombing, was a white supremacist who adhered to an accelerationist ideology. He also harbored deep anti-government sentiment, obsessing over convoluted conspiracy theories of government cover ups and lies, not dissimilar to the ideology seen in the Three Percenters and the Oath Keepers, anti-government groups that were present on January 6, 2021, and will be examined later in this chapter.

One of the chief influences on McVeigh—as well as many white supremacists today—was a novel called *The Turner Diaries*. First published in 1978, the book, by neo-Nazi William Luther Pierce (writing under the pseudonym Andrew Macdonald), tells the story of Earl Turner, who leads a group known as "the Organization" to bring about a revolution against the government, which is controlled by Jews and engages in extreme anti-white activity. Among the many actions of Turner's group is using a truck bomb to blow up FBI headquarters, and attacking the Capitol. In the book, the anti-government forces ultimately take control of the US government and commit mass-genocide against the non-white population, leading to the eventual creation of a blissful, white-dominated world.

In the more than forty years since its publication, the book has been cited as the rationale for numerous white supremacist attacks and hate crimes. As the *New York Times* wrote one week after the Oklahoma City bombing, "no other book has so influenced the culture of the extremist right."[1] The article also made the connection between the use of a truck bomb to destroy a federal building in the book and the Oklahoma City bombing before it was known that pages of *The Turner Diaries* were found in McVeigh's car.[2] Over twenty-five years later, the *Times* would write again about the continuing influence of *The Turner Diaries*, this time in the context of the attack on the Capitol.[3]

In addition to *The Turner Diaries*, McVeigh was also inspired to act in Oklahoma City by two other events that are at the forefront of modern-day domestic terrorism: Waco and Ruby Ridge.

Branch Davidians, as they were known, were members of a religious community living together in a settlement in Waco, Texas. The group followed the teachings of its enchanting leader, David Koresh. However, the peaceful religious solitude of the group was a façade. The group came to the attention of law enforcement after reports of Koresh taking child brides. He was also accused of stockpiling and illegally selling weapons.

In February 1993, federal law enforcement officials obtained an arrest warrant for Koresh and a search warrant for the compound where he and his followers lived. The execution of the warrants on February 28, 1993, did not go as planned, resulting in a shootout between Koresh's supporters and agents with the Bureau of Alcohol, Tobacco, and Firearms. Four agents and six Branch Davidians were killed. The shootout prompted additional law enforcement to surround the compound, leading to a standoff that would last nearly two months. On April 19, 1993, after a series of missteps by the FBI and others, the Branch Davidians set fire to their building. Seventy-five of them were killed in the blaze.

In the aftermath of Waco, the government received much criticism for its handling of the situation. While the incident did represent a significant overreach of government authority, rather than seeing it as a dark, one-off incident in American history, for extremists like McVeigh, it became the impetus for radicalization. His bombing of the federal building in Oklahoma City was, in his view, retaliation against a government he perceived to be oppressive and one that infringed upon the rights of its citizens. He even chose the date of the bombing, April 19, to correspond with the second anniversary of the end of the siege in Waco. In line with accelerationist thinking, McVeigh believed that the bombing in Oklahoma City would spark an uprising against the United States government, which in his view had slaughtered innocent Americans in the Texas desert.

Waco was not the only influence on McVeigh, and by extension, the militia and anti-government movement of today. Only six months earlier, in August 1992, US Marshals in Idaho tried to arrest Randy Weaver. A standoff ensured, which left Weaver's wife, his fourteen-year-old son, and a deputy marshal dead.

The standoff started with the government trying to

convince—or manipulate, depending on one's perspective—
Weaver to help them infiltrate local white supremacist groups.
After Weaver moved his family from Iowa to a home without
electricity or running water on an isolated mountaintop in
Idaho, he began following the Aryan Nations, a hate group that
was predominant in the area. A survivalist, against the system,
Weaver was cornered after the government charged him with
the illegal sale of a rifle. After he failed to appear in court on
the weapons charge, the government issued an arrest warrant,
but serving that warrant in Weaver's isolated mountain home
would prove to be difficult and dangerous. His son and the
US marshal would be the first to die, followed the next day
by Weaver's wife. These were grave mistakes on the part of the
government.

For those harboring anti-government sentiment, Ruby
Ridge, like Waco the following year, was proof that the
government had overstepped its reach, and was murdering
innocent women and children as it tried to take away the guns
of god-fearing Americans. Those on the far right saw Ruby
Ridge and Waco as examples of how the government could, in
their minds, come after them, without reason.

Militia groups used these two incidents as marketing and as
a recruitment tool. As the Southern Poverty Law Center highlighted, "militia groups, large and small, used the story of Ruby
Ridge to recruit people, to amplify existing anti-government
beliefs."[4] This created the perfect storm, and militia groups in

the United States exploded. Just three years later, the explosion would become literal in Oklahoma City.

After simmering underground during the early 2000s, the militia movement became more active with the election of Barack Obama. As the Center for Strategic & International Studies explained:

> Part of this revival stemmed from concerns over Democratic policy positions on issues such as gun control and immigration, as well as the strong reaction from white supremacist militia members to the prospect of having such policies established by the nation's first Black president. Moreover, the emergence of new mainstream political actors such as the Tea Party . . . offered perceived legitimacy to militias' ideas.[5]

Fast forward over a decade—which included the catalyzing election of Donald Trump in 2016—and by January 6, 2021, there was a prominent militia movement out in force to defend *their* president from what they saw as another example of extreme government overreach. The two most prominent groups in attendance that day were the Oath Keepers and the Three Percenters. Members of the Oath Keepers would later be convicted of seditious conspiracy, and the two groups would have a nearly equal number of members arrested for their roles in the insurrection, with 43 Oath Keepers and 39 Three Percenters charged.

Unlike many of the white supremacist groups or the Proud Boys, which were founded during the Trump presidency, the Oath Keepers have been around since 2009. Started by Elmer Stewart Rhodes III, who goes by Stewart Rhodes, the Oath Keepers believe that the US government is trying to strip its citizens of their rights. Rhodes is a Yale Law graduate and practiced law in Montana before being disbarred in 2015 for failure to appear for a disciplinary hearing.[6]

Beginning in 2014, the Oath Keepers couched themselves as protectors of freedom by providing services to individuals and causes they deemed in line with their beliefs, such as offering security at the Bundy Ranch after a dispute between a rancher and the Bureau of Land Management. The following year, the group showed up at the White Hope Mine, and later that same year, the Sugar Pine Mine, both of which were involved in disputes with the US government.[7] After the terrorist attack against a military recruitment center in Chattanooga in July 2015, the group started guarding recruitment centers in Tennessee and South Carolina.[8] During the Trump presidency, the Oath Keepers served as security guards to close Trump associates such as Roger Stone, Ali Alexander, Alex Jones, and Mike Flynn.[9] During Rhodes' seditious conspiracy trial in 2022 (he would be convicted and sentenced to eighteen years in prison, the longest term to date of anyone involved in the capitol riot), his attorney explained that the Oath Keepers were waiting for Trump to invoke the Insurrection Act,[10] a law that dates to the late 1700s and allows the president to use the military against United States citizens to maintain order.[11] In the aftermath of the 2020 election, the Oath Keepers began organizing in opposition to Biden's presidency, which included stockpiling weapons, and making plans to fight to get Trump back in office.[12]

Similar to other white supremacist groups, the Oath Keepers focus heavily on recruiting current and former members of the military and law enforcement. As the Anti-Defamation League concluded, "The group places a focus on seeking institutional power by specifically targeting current and former law enforcement, military, and emergency services personnel with their messaging and recruitment in the hopes that they will be able to utilize these unique skill sets to advance their cause . . ."[13]

In 2021, the Oath Keepers membership list was hacked and made public. It contained more than 38,000 names,* with nearly 500 belonging to current members of law enforcement

---

*. In the interest of full disclosure, my uncle, who has since passed away, appeared on the list. He, like many Oath Keepers, was a veteran and harbored deep anti-government sentiment. His beliefs were largely dismissed by the family and attributed to the severe mental health issues he had after returning from war. All were not surprised, but nonetheless disappointed, when I told them he was a dues-paying member of an extremist group.

and the military. More than eighty of the names on the list were individuals who had run for or been elected to public office. Among the elected officials was Arizona State Senator Wendy Rogers, who was the subject of an ethics investigation after posting on social media on May 14, 2022, that "fed boy summer has started in Buffalo."[14] "Fed boy summer" was a reference to the term "white boy summer," which has been adopted by white supremacist groups. It comes from an Instagram video and later rap by Chet Hanks, the son of actor Tom Hanks. The original music was not racist or political in nature, as Hanks clarified when the phrase was adopted by extremist groups, but it has since taken on a life of its own and is now more frequently associated with racists groups than with its originator.[15]

With that posting, Rogers was suggesting that the racist shooting committed by Peyton Gendron at a Buffalo supermarket involved the federal government. This, combined with Rogers unapologetically admitting she is a member of the Oath Keepers, reveals the dangerous intersection of extremism and politics between today's Republican Party and the white supremacist movement.

The other dominant militia contingent present at the Capitol attack was the Three Percenters.[16] The name is a reference to the false idea that only three percent of the colonists fought the British during the Revolutionary War. Like the Oath Keepers, the group believes that the government infringes upon its citizens' rights, and that armed individuals or militia have the right to overthrow an authoritarian government. Unlike the Oath Keepers, the Three Percenters are not a formal, structured group, but rather a collective of like-minded individuals who identify as right-wing and anti-government.

The Three Percenters concept was initiated by Mike Vanderboegh, who coined the term in a 2008 blog post. Vanderboegh, who died in 2016, was vehemently anti-government and wrote frequently about government conspiracies, with the Oklahoma City bombing being a particular topic of interest.[17]

Though nearly forty people who identified as Three Percenters were arrested for their action on January 6, 2021, this was not the first or only instance of the group engaging in violent behavior. In May 2020, a member of the Three Percenters plotted to kidnap and kill law enforcement officers in Ohio, intending to start an "uprising."[18] In 2017, five Three Percenters, who called their subgroup the "White Rabbits," planned a series of violent attacks including bombing a mosque, setting a women's health clinic on fire, killing a suspected drug trafficker and sabotaging railroad tracks in Illinois.[19]

Leading up to January 6, 2021, several Three Percenters chatted online, sharing information about the supposed election fraud in 2020 and coordinating their travel to Washington, DC. They discussed which hotels they'd stay in and the weapons they'd bring. On Telegram they established the "DC Brigade" where they explained how they would "organize a group of fighters to have each other's backs and ensure that no one will trample on our rights." Just after two on the afternoon of January 6, they pushed through the line of police officers, disparaging them as they pressed, and entered the Capitol through a broken window. "The people have taken back their house!" they declared upon entry.[20]

FIVE

The Big Lies

To date, over one thousand people have been charged with criminal offenses related to the January 6 insurrection. It may be surprising to some, but only about one-third of those charged were affiliated with an extremist group.[1] The rest were simply regular individuals, many influenced by conspiracy theories to believe that the 2020 election had been rigged in favor of Joe Biden, and therefore stolen from Donald Trump.

The "big lie,"[2] as the election conspiracy became known, had been perpetuated by Trump himself well before Election Day 2020. As far back as 2016, when Senator Ted Cruz won the Iowa Caucus, Trump cried foul, asserting that Cruz had "stolen" the caucus and committed "fraud."[3] Trump didn't like to lose, and his supporters followed suit. Many were at the Capitol on January 6 to right a perceived wrong, and to fight for their leader. They saw themselves as "lawful combatants" motivated by "a proposed plot carried out in secret ... by a powerful group of people who ha[d] some kind of sinister goal, with something to gain from what they're doing."[4] The "powerful group" included Democrats, the deep state, and others that the insurrectionists believed to be part of an elite cabal who secretly controlled the government.

Misinformation, disinformation, and *malinformation* are words frequently used to describe the "big lie," and, although often used interchangeably, they mean different things. *Misinformation* is false or inaccurate information, but the person or group disseminating that information believes it to be true. In other words, the spreading of the information is not necessarily done with the intent to mislead. These are your friends on Facebook who share outlandish political posts they fully believe to be the truth. This belief defines many of the insurrectionists on January 6. *Disinformation,* on the other hand, is inaccurate or false information that is distributed with the intent to mislead. The person or group or country distributing the information does so knowing it is false. Ahead of the 2020 election, misinformation often started as disinformation, planted by Trump's inner circle and foreign governments to sow doubt and discord. *Malinformation,* finally, is true information that is distributed with the intent to harm.

Many Trump supporters had lower levels of formal education, which made them susceptible to being misled. An analysis of voters in the 2016 election found that the majority of those who voted for Trump did not have a college degree.[5] As one researcher explained, "People with lower levels of education tend to be drawn to conspiracy theories. And we don't argue that's because people are not intelligent. It's simply that they haven't been allowed to have or haven't been given access to the tools to allow them to differentiate between good sources and bad sources or credible sources and non-credible sources."[6] Trump was acutely aware of who his base was and exploited their gullibility and lack of critical thinking skills for his personal gain.

While many of the participants on January 6 were enchanted by the big lie, others were persuaded to believe more eccentric claims. Principal among them were QAnon adherents, who believed that the government was controlled by Democratic politicians as well as some media personalities and Hollywood-types, all of whom were Satan-worshipping pedophiles, led by Hillary Clinton and Nancy Pelosi. There were 105 QAnon adherents arrested for their activities on January 6, more than any other group.[7]

The tale of devil-worshippers controlling the government came from a single email. In March 2016, John Podesta, former White House Chief of Staff under Bill Clinton, was the victim of a phishing scam. Podesta was sent a message asking him to change his password. He complied, unwittingly giving a hacker access to his emails. One message from his brother invited him and Hillary Clinton to attend a dinner hosted by the artist Marina Abramović, to raise money for her charitable foundation. At the dinner party, guests were asked to make soup, which Abramović called "spirit cooking." According to QAnon, it was not soup they were preparing, but a cauldron brewing. Abramović was also known to use blood in her artwork, lending believability to stories of the occult. Neither John Podesta nor Hillary Clinton attended the party, but the invite was enough to start the rumor that they and many others worshipped Satan.[8]

QAnon was started in October 2017 by an anonymous user named Q, who posted on the social media platform 4chan.[*, 9, 10] Some of QAnon's "drops"—the word used to describe pieces of information Q fed to his followers—were intentionally vague, and drew on already well-established conspiracies, allowing followers to weave their own closely held fringe beliefs into

---

[*]. 4chan is an online chat forum where the posters are anonymous. The threads are also "pruned," or automatically expire, after a certain period of time. As someone who had to research threats against elected officials, the message board was a challenge. Due to the nature of 4chan, it was very difficult for law enforcement to identify who was making the threats without a subpoena.

Christopher Poole created the forum in 2003, and it was later purchased by Hiroyuki Nishimura. There are chat rooms and imageboards on a variety of topics, some of which are benign, such as manga and anime boards, but many are depraved. While supporters applaud the platform for its free speech ideals and its lack of content policies and moderation, 4chan is a bastion of misogyny, racism, abuse, and hate. The platform has hosted images of child pornography, threats against historically Black colleges and universities, and other harmful material.

a larger narrative. (Several of Q's early "drops" pertained to Hillary Clinton and the Democratic Party.) Q claimed to be a government insider working for the US military, who was privy to government secrets. Q was later identified to be at least two people: Paul Furber and Ron Watkins, though Watkins denies this. Watkins would later run for Congress and lose.[11] Both were relatively obscure techy types, with Watkins developing 8kun, a social media platform similar to 4chan, and Furber being a South African software developer.

The followers of Q committed many unlawful acts long before they stormed the Capitol. In 2018, one follower blocked a road near the Hoover Dam in the name of "patriotism."[12] In 2019, another follower shot a member of the Gambino crime family believing he was a member of the deep state.[13] When it looked like Trump might lose the election in 2020, QAnon lent itself to perpetuating election fraud conspiracies. While individually there was purpose in these conspiracies, they also created an "overinflated sense of importance" for the followers when they were part of a group.[14] As they broke windows and beat officers on January 6, QAnon adherents were filled with a sense of self-importance, believing they were saving the country.

QAnon has received much attention since it started, partly driven by its huge explosion in followers, moving from a small group on social media to being a mainstream force that undermined our democracy in very real and threatening ways.

What the founders of QAnon did well, to the detriment of this country, was to take theories that had been drifting about in the online universe pertaining to political figures, the pandemic, and the election, and bound them together to become a force.

In many ways, QAnon was influenced by Alex Jones, who, twenty years earlier, began his own personal disinformation quest with *InfoWars*.

Started as a public access show in Texas in 1999, *InfoWars* hawked conspiracies about government weather control, mass shootings, the New World Order, and other fringe topics. The show expanded to radio and grew exponentially in popularity. At its height in the mid-2010s, *InfoWars* was generating millions of dollars a year in sales from advertisements, merchandise, and the products Jones promoted on the show. The program exploded on social media before most of the mainstream outlets banned it from their platforms. A huge supporter of Trump, Jones was a speaker at the MAGA I and II rallies and provided funding for the January 6 rally.[15] In 2022, after vehemently insisting that the Sandy Hook school shooting that killed twenty young children and six adults was a hoax, Jones was found guilty of defamation and was ordered to pay more than one billion dollars in damages.

Conspiracy theories are often prevalent in what are known as "societal crisis situations." Researchers Jan Willem van Prooijen and Karen M. Douglas define a societal crisis situation as "impactful and rapid societal change that calls established power structures, norms of conduct, or even the existence of specific people or groups into question."[16] These types of situations help explain longtime conspiracies like those pertaining to the JFK assassination, or 9/11.

In the past few years, COVID lockdowns and the way they reshaped our lives led to an unprecedented number of people engaging with medical conspiracies and ideas of government control. Locked away in our homes for months, we all suffered under the pandemic's isolation, fear, and strain on our mental health. People turned to the internet for explanations, information, and social interaction; "conspiracy theories appear to be driven by motives such as understanding one's environment, being safe and in control of one's environment, and maintaining a positive image of the self and the social group."[17] It should then come as no surprise that groups of similar-minded individuals were conversing online and whipping themselves into a conspiracy theory-fueled frenzy. Conspiracies have always offered easy explanations to complex problems. They give believers a feeling of control in a world that seems chaotic, and also provide them with a sense of community.

I have seen firsthand how conspiracy theories can directly impact a family. My cousin, whom I adored as a child, has fallen deep into the rabbit hole of political delusions. Her social media is filled with post after post criticizing favorites of the far-right such as Hillary Clinton and Nancy Pelosi, while raining praise on the likes of Donald Trump. For me, the final straw was when she posted a meme that said, "Democrats have proven they don't love their children." I told her I was a Democrat and loved my children. As someone who'd grown up with me, I naively assumed she'd know me well enough to agree. Not so. Her response? "I'm sorry the truth hurts." I had to block her on social media. As someone who has seen firsthand the violence conspiracies can cause, it hurt me on multiple levels to see a family member believe and promote such obvious untruths.

All of this is not just a recent trend. At the beginning of the twentieth century, there was a spike in conspiracy theories, which corresponded to the second industrial revolution, a period of significant and relatively quick societal change. The conspiracies of the time often had to do with banks controlling businesses and the distribution of wealth. In the 1950s, with the dawn of the Cold War, conspiracies also flourished.[18]

January 6, 2021, was also not the first instance in United States history where conspiracies and scandals made their way into a presidential election. Used as a weapon, conspiracies and disinformation have been persuasive elements in presidential campaigns as far back as the 1820s. In the 1824 election, John Quincy Adams won the most electoral college votes. However, he did not win the popular vote—just like Trump in 2016—prompting one of his opponents, Andrew Jackson, to call for the elimination of the electoral college. There were five candidates in that election, with Jackson receiving more electoral and popular votes than all the other candidates except for Adams. But, because Adams didn't win the majority of the electoral votes, the election was forced to a runoff with Jackson, Adams, and a third candidate, Henry Clay. The runoff resulted in Adams winning, with Jackson claiming that Clay had conspired with Adams to draw votes away from him.

Four years later, Adams and Jackson were again paired in the presidential election. This time Jackson won, but both sides used conspiracy theories to motivate voters, attempting to erode the trust Americans had in the electoral process.

During his re-election campaign in 1832, conspiracy theorists held that Jackson was a member of the ruling elite, supported by the Freemasons. Adding to the intrigue, an individual who had threatened to divulge secrets about the organization had been murdered a few years earlier. This prompted a group known as the Anti-Masons to support an opponent who was rumored to be associated with Henry Clay, to run against Jackson. Supporters of Jackson declared that there was a "deep laid conspiracy to defeat the wishes of the people."[19]

During his second term, Jackson took aim at the Second Bank of the United States, which served as the chief financial institution of the United States at the time. Jackson and his followers circulated disinformation saying that the president of the bank had used deposits, which consisted of both public and private monies, to fund and support Adams' previous presidential campaign.[20] This prompted the bank to take actions to pressure the government, which ultimately resulted in a recession. This in turn generated even more conspiracies about secret aristocrats controlling the bank.[21]

In 1835, there was an assassination attempt against Jackson. The would-be shooter was rumored to have been affiliated with Senator George Poindexter of Mississippi, a staunch opponent of Jackson. Others countered that the assassination attempt was staged to garner support for the president, who had clashed with "Slave Power," which was a reference to Southern elites who had a vested interest in expanding slavery throughout the United States. Conspiracy theorists later postulated that Slave Power was not only behind the assassination attempt on Jackson, but also had a hand in the deaths of president's William Henry Harrison, who died of pneumonia thirty-two days after becoming president in 1841, and Zachary Taylor, who passed away after a short illness in 1850.[22]

While conspiracy theories have long existed, more recently they've become part of the political mainstream. Prior to her first congressional victory, Representative Marjorie Taylor

Greene said that her election was "a once-in-a-lifetime opportunity to take this global cabal of Satan-worshipping pedophiles out."[23] On December 11, 2021, Representative Lauren Boebert tweeted that, "365,348 children went missing in 2020. You haven't heard a word from the media about it. There enlies [sic] the problem," implying they were abducted, an allusion to the QAnon belief that Democrats and other elites were trafficking children for illicit purposes. Boebert later deleted the tweet.[24]

Conspiracy theories reached the highest levels of the government during the Trump administration. While running for president in 2016, Trump promoted the idea that Barack Obama's birth certificate was fake. To discredit Senator Ted Cruz, Trump claimed that Cruz's father had ties to Lee Harvey Oswald. He also promoted the false belief that Jeffrey Epstein didn't commit suicide. As his presidency progressed, the conspiracies continued. Antifa was responsible for the Buffalo supermarket shooting. Global warming was a lie.

On January 6, there was a belief that martial law would be declared by military leaders and that Biden and many other Democratic politicians would be arrested and Trump would be reinstated as leader of the United States. This *Star Wars*-esque "Clone Protocol 66" plan was known as "The Storm" in QAnon circles. According to the group's adherents, Trump needed to be the leader of the free world because only he could eliminate the threat that Democrats and other deep state actors posed to the nation's children. To those who believed, Trump would bring about "The Great Awakening."

Except he didn't.

SIX

What Should Have Happened Next

Without any assistance from the former director, Norm Grahe, I was left on my own to try to figure out how things worked within the Intelligence and Interagency Coordination Division (IICD) of the Capitol Police. This would have been difficult even under normal circumstances, but these were far from normal circumstances. Outside my window stood protesters upset with Amy Comey Barrett, Trump's pick for the Supreme Court. There was a contentious election just days away. And within the walls of my building, I was up against an under-performing team that I was struggling to motivate at a time when I needed them the most.

In addition to the election, my team was also dealing with thousands of threats against members of Congress. The Capitol Police used techniques that searched certain keywords and terms related to threats on mainstream social media sites. When the system found something suspicious, it sent an alert via email to everyone on the team. In a highly functioning team, this would have been fine, but with the team I had, unless a task was assigned to a specific person, it was unlikely to be worked on.

To try and correct this, I set up a dedicated email for these alerts and sent out instructions on how to process them. I tasked someone with monitoring the email box, to make sure these threats were being assigned and investigated. Instead, the alerts piled up—hundreds of them, all potential threats against members of Congress, or against the Capitol itself.

In the end, I was left to go through the email box myself and assign out the alerts, ten at a time, to each analyst. This was not well received—some of the analysts resented the fact they were being asked to work threat cases. On one occasion, an analyst asked me to tell them what a threat was. However, it wasn't lost on me that what they were really asking was if *I* knew what a threat was. After working as an intelligence analyst for well over a decade, I knew that this person understood a threat when they saw one. "All of you are analysts and in reading these alerts, I trust you'll be able to recognize a threat," I responded. "Again, if there is a question about a particular alert, please feel free to reach out."[1]

Many of the analysts who were unhappy with me would later say I had pulled them away from collecting intelligence ahead of the insurrection. In reality, we still had other time-sensitive work that needed to be completed. We couldn't be singularly focused because the workload wouldn't allow it.

Even when I was trying to help define threats, it seemed to cause outrage. For example, a member of Congress feared she was being targeted by a transnational gang after calling out the corrupt president of a Central American country on social media. Transnational gangs were not something the Capitol Police routinely encountered, so I offered to have someone from Immigration and Custom Enforcement give us a briefing. This was embraced by the Investigations Division, which was looking into the threat.

However, some members of my team didn't feel the same way. After setting up the briefing and inviting members of IICD to attend, one analyst called me. "I used to work with gangs all the time," the person said, their voice raised, clearly upset that they weren't being asked to work on the threat. However, this analyst hadn't worked with gangs in years, and I found it unlikely they had done any research or had had any discussions about transnational gangs since joining the Capitol Police. "The people from ICE have the most current knowledge on the topic," I responded. "I did a lot of work with gangs in my last job, but I'd still prefer that we bring in the subject matter experts to do the briefing. They deal with this topic every day; the briefers have been to El Salvador to learn more about the gangs. Have you been to El Salvador?"

"No! Have you?!" the person snarled.

"Yeah, actually I have, but I'd still prefer that ICE do the briefing."

"I understand transitions are hard, but this one is bumpier than most," one of my team members said to me over the phone. I shifted in the chair at my desk, running my fingers through my hair. All my supervisory and leadership training had not adequately prepared me for the challenges I now faced. As we monitored the intelligence pertaining to the upcoming MAGA rallies, I could see that a significant portion of my team were resistant to the changes I was trying to implement—changes that I approached with urgency because of the charged political atmosphere.

As I continued conversing with the person on the other end of the phone—whom I had never met in person—I grew more concerned about how I was going to get my team to the place I needed it to be. I agreed with the team member about the rockiness of my transition, but I believed that the tension was the product of the need to improve the performance of the team versus the team's desire not to change the way it had been doing things for years.

Several members of my team also became upset when I issued performance standards to all the intelligence analysts. Performance forms for the fiscal year were usually issued in September; however, in December, Human Resources notified me that none of the forms had been issued to anyone on my team. I used this as an opportunity, including the performance standards used by other federal agencies in the executive branch of the government. Prior to me including these standards, the actions that analysts were required to take to meet expectations in each core competency had never been communicated to them.

Several members of my team saw the inclusion of performance standards as an overstep of my authority. One person, who was later placed on a Performance Improvement Plan, or PIP, at the end of the rating period the following year, complained that "AD Farnam changed all of the Core Competencies for PECS* appraisal established in USCP Directive 1053.18, and then issued appraisal to [intelligence analysts] of not meeting the standard . . . My PECS appraisal was completed with violations of USCP policy and regulations, to include abuse of power by changing the core competencies . . ."[2] In truth, I hadn't changed the core competencies; they were the same ones that had always been on the form. I had simply added descriptions of what an employee had to do to meet the expectations in each competency. Those descriptions had been cleared by the Capitol Police's Office of Chief Counsel before they were issued to the analysts. Without the descriptions, there was nothing to measure whether someone was meeting a core competency.

But while I was trying to assess the performance of my team, I was never issued a performance form or appraisal myself during my time at the USCP. Not having one made it

---

*. The Performance Evaluation and Communication System (PECS) is the form the Capitol Police uses to document performance.

challenging for me when I wanted to leave the USCP. This was unbelievable to most employers because it is standard practice in nearly every professional organization, both public and private. The message that was sent by not issuing me an appraisal and not including any sort of benchmarks or expectations for the analysts was that that performance wasn't a priority for the Capitol Police, at least not for civilian employees.

My team weren't the only ones experiencing internal tensions in the weeks leading up to January 6, 2021. On the other side of the ledger, there was a falling out between Cindy Chafian and Women for America First (WFAF). Chafian had been the primary organizer on behalf of the organization for the MAGA I and II rallies at Freedom Plaza, and she also held the permit for the next rally that was to take place at the Plaza, scheduled for January 6. The rumor mill around Washington said that the conflict between Chafian and WFAF had to do with who had a seat on a bus in a caravan that had traveled to the MAGA II rally. More likely, it had to do with money and creative differences.[3] For her part, Chafian told ProPublica that she was pushed aside as plans for the January 6 rally developed.[4] This may have been true, but Chafian also had a vested interest in distancing herself from the insurrection.

In the meetings we had with Chafian leading up to January 6, she made several snide comments about the organizers of the Ellipse event that was also scheduled for that day, and was very obviously angry toward Women for America First. The pettiness between Chafian and WFAF was apparent in an email Chafian sent to the National Park Service on December 28, 2020:

> I don't want there to be any confusion with regard to the application and it's come to my attention that my former client is claiming that the application belongs to them ... I was clear in all of the text messages that the application was mine and in my name. Women for America First failed to respond to any requests for information via text message. They failed to answer or respond to any of my calls.[5]

In the email, Chafian was trying to make the case that the permit for Freedom Plaza was hers—not Women for America First. WFAF stated the opposite, that the permit belonged to them and not the person who was planning the rally on its behalf.

The final break between the two happened abruptly. Between the MAGA II rally on December 12 and late December, Chafian was still communicating with the National Park Service on behalf of WFAF. On December 21, 2020, Chafian notified the National Park Service that the permit would be under her name and not Women for America First. She also said that the official name of the event would be "Rally to Save America."[6] The name would eventually be changed to

"Rally to Revival," likely to not be confused with Women for America First's "Save America" rally.

Ultimately, Chafian got a permit for 5,000 participants at Freedom Plaza. Women for America First didn't put up much of a fight because they didn't have to, as they got the Ellipse *and* the president at their rally.

Following the MAGA II rally, Capitol Police Deputy Chief Sean Gallagher asked Jack Donohue and I how many people had been arrested in the city related to the protest. Jack responded that he'd check with Lieutenant Shane Lamond, the intelligence head at the Metropolitan Police Department (MPD).

I envied Jack's connections and, more than that, resented that he didn't bring me into the fold. He never introduced me to the people he knew. I couldn't help thinking that I wasn't part of Jack's circle because I wasn't a cop, and I was a woman. Men always start at a place of credibility; women always start with having no credibility. This in turn means that women have to work twice as hard just to make it to the male starting line. This is especially true in male-dominated professions like law enforcement and intelligence. Jack would attend meetings on the Hill and not include me. When he'd return from these meetings, he wouldn't share what was discussed. He sent emails, and received responses, from Capitol Police leadership, but didn't think it important enough for me to know the contents.

Some evenings, he'd leave the office early to attend happy hour with other cops he knew. I was never invited.

Jack always talked about Shane, who was known as the go-to person for law enforcement intelligence in Washington. Shane knew everyone, and everyone knew Shane. Except me. Based on how Jack spoke about him, I thought they had known each other for years. I later discovered they had communicated infrequently over email when Jack was still at the NYPD and had only met a couple times before Jack was hired by the Capitol Police. Their relationship seemed to be based on them being part of the cop network that I couldn't figure out how to break into. I was not allowed to reach out directly to Shane without Jack's permission. Jack made it clear to me that Shane was his territory by saying that he was the one who would check with Shane on issues like the intelligence MPD was tracking, information about demonstrations in Washington, and meetings they were planning. I felt purposely excluded.

When Shane sent out an email inviting everyone to a holiday party, I responded that I would attend, surprised to have even been invited. I answered quickly, in the hopes the invite wasn't an accident. I finally would get to meet all the people Jack carried on about and purported to know so well. Like a bandit looking for loot, this was my opportunity to get on the inside. These were people I needed to network with and build relationships with if I was to be successful in my role at IICD. If I couldn't go to them because Jack was the roadblock, then I'd get them to come to me. I had to be affable and have them trust me, and I had to build that bridge so they would communicate with me directly. And I had to make friends with Shane so I wouldn't be dependent on Jack for information.

On the day of the party, Jack had to travel to New York and wasn't going to be able to make it. I was secretly ecstatic he wouldn't be able to attend, as I would be able to make myself known independently and wouldn't be standing in anyone's shadow.

I planned out what I would wear—my red and white striped top with the boat neck and a short black skirt that flared at the bottom—and thought about what I'd talk about. I had conversations in my head with these people before I'd even met them.

When I arrived at the restaurant, I looked around and didn't see any organized groups. I asked the hostess if there were any holiday parties. She said there was one in the room to the left and another one in the back. I walked into the first room, which was filled with older men who looked like they could have once been in a biker gang. They were wearing leather vests, jeans, boots, long gray beards and bandannas. This obviously wasn't my party. I left the room and headed toward the room at the back of the restaurant. There I saw several tall men, their hair cut short, their faces clean shaven, loud and boisterous with drinks in hand. These were my people.

Although I was determined to be outgoing, walking into a

room full of people I didn't know was uncomfortable. I was on my own. But I had a job to do. My objectives: drink one beer, be friendly, pass out my business cards, and then head for the door.

"Are any of you Shane?" I said to a group of men.

"I'm Shane," one answered. I should have guessed. He was standing in the middle of everyone, toward the back of the small room. He was about six feet tall, dark hair shaved close to the head, olive skin, with a pronounced dimple in his chin.

Before I had an opportunity to say anything to him, another man came up to me, "Get you a beer?" The man brought me over a beer, and I ended up talking to him and a few others for a while. Everyone there was a current or former cop, except for two wives accompanying their spouses. Including me, there were only three women at the party. I was the only woman who actually worked with these men.

As I drank my beer, I put up with the usual actions of intoxicated men—putting their arm around me, lewd comments, and other actions that I could handle, but shouldn't have to. I made the rounds and met everyone in the room. Once I figured that I had made my mark, I got ready to leave. As I gathered my coat, Shane came up to me. We shared some inconsequential pleasantries but did exchange phone numbers.

Within fifteen minutes of my departing the bar, Shane texted to say that he had enjoyed meeting me, and sent me a friend request on Facebook. A couple days after that, he asked if I'd like to meet him for drinks. I politely declined, saying I had plans, though I did not. I didn't want to go out with him, but I did want him to like and trust me. He asked again a few days later. I again said no. Soon after the new year began, he asked me yet again. This time I said yes. Maybe it was better this way, I rationalized. I'd have a drink with him and then be on my way. We planned to meet on January 7.

But before then, there would be other things to deal with.

For the first two MAGA rallies, the Capitol Police were prepared only because nothing out of the ordinary happened. For the November rally, participants gathered in Freedom Plaza, standing shoulder to shoulder on the cold concrete, wearing their trademark red MAGA caps, American flags draped across their shoulders as capes. They marched down the National Mall and gathered at the steps of the Supreme Court, listening to several speakers. And then they dispersed without fanfare. That evening, off Capitol grounds, there were skirmishes between the Proud Boys, antifa, and others, but the Capitol Police were not involved. The second rally was much the same, with the exception that people gathered at the Supreme Court first and then marched to Freedom Plaza. With both of those rallies, the intelligence did not suggest violence, though we were mindful of the extremists in attendance.

The intelligence indicated that the January 6 rally would be far different, which my division communicated to the Capitol Police leadership. Despite our warnings, they couldn't comprehend that January 6 would be unlike the first two MAGA rallies. This was a failure of leadership. Perhaps it was because of the Capitol Police's experiences with the two previous Stop the Steal events that they didn't think that anything violent would happen on January 6. The intelligence assessment I wrote on January 3 noted that the rally on the sixth would be similar in size to the first two MAGA rallies—a sentence that was erroneously interpreted as saying that it would be just like the first two MAGA rallies.

Therefore, the Capitol Police prepared for January 6 like it was any other protest. Indeed, an IT professional who visited then Capitol Police Chief Stephen Sund's office on the morning of the sixth asked him how he thought the day would go. Sund responded that he "didn't expect it to be too bad."[7] There was no acknowledgment that known far-right groups, under the Stop the Steal banner, were planning to come to the Capitol.

Another law enforcement group that was ill equipped for January 6 was the National Guard. General Charles Flynn— brother of the disgraced Michael Flynn—was deputy chief of staff for Army operations on January 6. Sources within the Department of Defense reported that Flynn's actions were part of the reason why the military was unprepared and reluctant to assist on January 6.[8]

The head of intelligence for Army Headquarters was

briefed days before the insurrection. A report, written by an ad hoc team consisting of members of G-2 (Intelligence) and G-3 (Operations) and provided to General Flynn and Major General Bradley Gericke, outlined the possibility of violence from the far right on January 6, 2021. The potential for disorder was so great, the recommendation was to posture military assets to be ready to respond if necessary. Both Flynn and Gericke were dismissive of the report and explicitly stated it should have contained more information about antifa.[9] There was a disinclination to call in the National Guard to protect the Capitol by many people for various reasons, but the lack of preparedness in part sat within the Department of Defense and largely with Michael Flynn's brother.

The consequence of this disregarding of the intelligence was that the National Guard was not at the ready when it was needed most. By General Flynn's own admission, the DC National Guard, as well as National Guard assets from Maryland, Virginia, and Pennsylvania, which would supplement the DC National Guard through a compact agreement, were not prepared to respond to a riot. Though Flynn categorized National Guard assistance as a "last resort," he was provided with information that even if a last resort, the National Guard was likely to have been needed on January 6.[10]

When Secretary of the Army Ryan McCarthy testified that "the intelligence that [DoD] received was that there was no real major difference" between the January 6, 2021, event and the previous two MAGA marches,[11] he very well could have believed that to be true, but that belief was only possible because intelligence that indicated otherwise had been deliberately withheld from him by Flynn and Gericke. It was more than just a question of optics; it was a disregard for the overwhelming intelligence that obstructed the military's preparedness when it was needed to protect our democracy.

Between December 16, 2020, the date the January 6 rally was announced publicly, and January 3, 2021, there were three iterations of the intelligence assessment authored by my team. The assessments evolved as more intelligence was collected, but the Capitol Police's planning did not. The premise of the rally on January 6 was materially different than the MAGA I and II rallies—no one was waiting for a state to declare their election results, and the court challenges had largely been dismissed— and that difference should have been key in how the Capitol Police prepared for the crowds.

This distinction between the MAGA rallies made it clear that the groups on January 6 were going to focus on Congress and the Capitol. When I said in my intelligence assessment, "Congress itself is the target," it was simple logic. Like Faulkner describing Dewey Dell's belly full of child, her "wet dress shapes for the dead eyes of three blind men those mammalian ludicrosities which are the horizons and the valleys of the earth," so too was the Capitol Police blind to a day pregnant with the possibility of disaster.

Writing the intelligence assessments had not been a straightforward process. Initially I assigned the drafting of the assessment for the January 6 rally to an analyst who would be transferred off my team in the immediate aftermath of the insurrection. Reading what they had turned in, it was apparent that I had my work cut out for me. The document contained numerous grammatical mistakes, the intelligence referenced was scattered in a hodgepodge way and the analysis section was inarticulate.

"You rewrote the whole thing," Jack Donohue said to me when I finally sent him the assessment.

"The original document wasn't ready for primetime. We need to do better than that."

This was the December 16, 2020, version of the assessment, which was never distributed. It should be noted that the first mentions of violence related to January 6 did not come until days later, so this version of the assessment did not discuss the possibility of violence because there was no intelligence to support that conclusion. Permits for the events on the Ellipse and Freedom Plaza also had not yet been filed.

I sent a rewritten version of the assessment, dated December 23, 2020, to Sean Gallagher, but that document was provided to only a handful of others in the Capitol Police. Soon thereafter, as the date of the MAGA III rally (as we were calling it then) approached, I reassigned the task of writing the intelligence assessment to another analyst. I had them start from scratch because I wanted to see if the intelligence they collected differed from the information already in hand. Right or wrong, I did not disclose to the analyst that someone else on the team had already written an assessment, albeit an awful one. The second analyst returned a document equally as disappointing as the first, with limited information from any fringe social media sites and ultimately concluding that most of the protesters would be peaceful.

For the final version of the intelligence assessment that was distributed on January 3, 2021, I took some of what the first two analysts had written, information received from intelligence and law enforcement partners, as well as items I had located myself. The assessment wasn't perfect and there is a lot I wish had been done better.

Here are some of what I believe to be valid criticisms of the assessment.

First, the Office of Inspector General of the Capitol Police later made a recommendation to improve the Bottom-Line Up Front (BLUF) in the intelligence assessment. A BLUF is common in many intelligence products and provides the most salient points of the assessment at the top of the document. I largely agree with this recommendation, though I will point out that the BLUF didn't completely miss its mark. It stated, ". . . some protesters have indicated they plan to be armed. There is also indication that white supremacist groups may be attending the protests." Those sentences appeared at the top of the first page. It is also important to note that not even two months earlier the whole Intelligence and Interagency Coordination Division had never heard of, or used, a BLUF.

The second criticism was a section of the assessment that was interpreted to mean that MAGA III would be the same as the first two MAGA marches. On page two of the assessment, I wrote:

> The protests/rallies are expected to be similar to the previous Million MAGA March rallies in November and December 2020, which drew tens of thousands of participants. It is also expected that members of the Proud Boys, Antifa, and other extremist groups will rally on January 6, 2021. Multiple arrests were made as a result of clashes between pro-Trump and opposing groups during each of the November and December rallies. Charges included assault with a dangerous weapon, assault on police, simple assault, weapons violations, riotous acts, destruction of property, disorderly conduct, resisting arrest, and crossing a police line. A number of law enforcement officers were injured in the skirmishes.[12]

Those who read the first sentence of that paragraph may have assumed that the January rally would be just like those in November and December, though much of the remainder of the assessment emphasized worrisome intelligence on how January 6 was going to be unlike the previous two MAGA rallies. I could have phrased that first sentence differently to avoid any confusion.

The next sentences that I felt were misinterpreted appeared on page five of the assessment: "IICD has identified more than forty social media postings promoting protests on January 6, 2021. The number of people who indicate they are going to the event listed on these social media postings is relatively low." This statement is accurate. Each individual who posted on social media listed only a few people as going to the rally, interested, liking, etc. However, adding up all those individual postings—in addition to those who were planning to come but weren't on social media—did add up to numbers in the thousands, similar to the attendance at the first and second MAGA rallies. Those sentences were not intended to mean that only a few people would be coming to the rally on January 6, but that was how some interpreted them.

The final assessment also contained a lengthy section on street closures in Washington, DC, for January 6. I agree with the critique that the traffic information shouldn't have been included in the assessment. However, I had been asked to add it because traffic was a significant concern for Capitol Police leadership in the run up to the sixth. On Tuesday—the day before the insurrection—I explicitly asked if the National

Guard would be called in. The response I received was, "They'll be helping with traffic cuts and street closures." It wasn't my choice to include road closure information in the assessment.

Capitol Police Chief Steven Sund asserted he didn't take the intelligence seriously because the overall analysis piece, which appeared at the end of the assessment, was "peppered with qualifiers."[13] Intelligence is not clairvoyance. Neither I, nor anyone, can say with certainty what the future will hold. When I wrote, "violence cannot be ruled out" and "there is the possibility that protesters may be inclined to become violent," it was done with the intent to alert Capitol Police leadership of the potential for danger. When I said it "may lead to a significantly dangerous situation," it was my expectation that leadership would prepare for a significantly dangerous situation. (After all, I didn't say it would be peaceful.) Sund also said that final paragraph in the assessment "only added confusion,"[14] yet he never asked for clarification about its contents.

On January 4, 2021, the Capitol Police leadership were invited to a briefing about the demonstration planned for two days later, but many did not attend. (The invitation was for those officials with a rank of captain and above.) Though I didn't send the invite and I didn't know who was on the call, I understood during the briefing that participation was limited. Chief Sund was not on the call. While he was inadvertently left off the invite, Sean Gallagher had sent him an email the day before notifying him of the briefing.[15] Sund showed little interest in attending, or the contents of what was discussed. He didn't follow up when he didn't get the invite, nor did he ask to be back briefed.

Ultimately, while the intelligence assessment was not perfect, IICD did produce a report that sounded the alarm about what could happen on January 6. In Sund's book, *Courage Under Fire*, he wrote that, "Farnam was hired at the recommendation and insistence of Pittman and Gallagher . . . [The Select Committee] kept returning to the fiction that since I was the chief and hence the final hiring authority, I had personally selected those who were at the center of the intelligence failure . . ."[16] However, the only reason there was accurate intelligence available to the USCP leadership in advance of the insurrection was because of my presence on the team. Not only did IICD author an assessment, but I personally wrote the most integral part of it. If I hadn't done that, no one else would have.

SEVEN

January 6, 2021

They chanted, "USA! USA! USA!" before jerking the bike racks away from the police officers. Seconds later the punches started, and then thick yellow streams of bear spray were showering the officers, coating their uniforms and faces with a noxious dust. A struggle ensued, eventually breaching the line. Like a plague of locusts, they poured over the ground and up to the Capitol building. Bang! Crack! The man in the black cap with a Gadsden rattlesnake embroidered on the front slammed the end of an American flag into the terrace window. With the thud of the flagpole and the roar of the crowd, he shattered more than glass. The mob then made its way into the Capitol building. And like the *Book of Exodus* said of the locusts, the world was witnessing "something neither your fathers nor your forefathers have ever seen from the day they settled into this land until now."[1]

I arrived at work around eight o'clock on the morning of January 6, 2021. It was a cloudy day, though not too cold. We were all hoping for frigid temperatures and snow to keep the protesters away, but it was not to be. Driving down D Street to my office, I had seen several cars decked out in anti-Chinese, anti-communist signs. This group made regular appearances around the Hill, as they wanted Congress to declare the Chinese Communist Party a terrorist organization. However, this was not the day to make a political point about a foreign country—the United States and its own internal issues would be front and center on the world stage.

As I approached the door to my building, I saw a group of Proud Boys walking across the street. I chuckled to myself because the group had been buzzing all over social media about how its members should dress incognito for the march, no black shirts with yellow writing, no roosters or laurel wreaths, as was their typical attire. However, before me were several members donned in their usual clothing. I wore red so I could blend into the crowd if need be.

The first email I sent was at 8:01 AM. There had been a gang of protesters outside Senator Mitch McConnell's house and I needed my team to monitor them in case things got out of hand. At the time, McConnell received more threats and was the subject of more concerning comments than any other member of Congress. Unlike Speaker Pelosi or other high-profile figures on either side of the aisle, McConnell not only upset liberals, but the far-right hated him, too. Trump didn't help matters, as he was constantly barraging the soon-to-be minority leader with insults.

The main events of the day were supposed to take place at the Ellipse, which is located near the White House, and at Freedom Plaza. Both places are about a mile and a half from the Capitol Building. Although most of the activities weren't supposed to start until late morning, except for a scheduled prayer service at 9:00 AM at Freedom Plaza, that part of the city was already crowded. Trump was scheduled to speak around noon at the Ellipse.

I settled in at my desk and called Shane Lamond, who was down at Freedom Plaza, to get an estimate of the crowd size. Since meeting him the month before at the holiday party, we texted regularly. He was flirty and charming. He'd ask about my day, and he started including me on emails he sent to other officials. I now felt comfortable enough to pick up the phone and call him. The following night would be our first date, and I was looking forward to it.

He estimated there were about 25,000 people at the Plaza, a figure I reported to Yogananda Pittman, then the Capitol Police's Assistant Chief for Protection and Intelligence Operations.[2] She oversaw the Protective Services Bureau, of which IICD was a part. I also received information from the Washington Metropolitan Area Transit Authority abut public transportation ridership. On weekdays during the pandemic, daily ridership was approximately 86,000. As of noon on January 6, 2021, the ridership was already at 60,000; it would reach over 132,000 by the end of the day.[3] I knew that this increase was people coming to the MAGA rally, and I knew they were coming for Congress.

At 10:00 AM, Deputy Chief Sean Gallagher, the head of the Protective Services Bureau, who reported directly to Pittman, called a meeting for leadership within the Bureau. The Protective Services Bureau includes three divisions—IICD, the Investigations Division and the Dignitary Protection Division. As mentioned earlier, the Investigations Division is responsible for criminal investigations of threats against members of Congress and other similar activity (e.g., office break-ins, etc.). The Investigations Division is also responsible for counter-surveillance at events. On January 6, all the Task Force Officers—agents assigned to other agencies such as the FBI—fell under the Investigations Division (post-insurrection, the Capitol Police leadership realigned them to be under me at IICD). Dignitary Protection was like the Secret Service of the Capitol, providing security to congressional leadership, among others.*

No one from the Uniformed Services Bureau, which includes nearly all the officers in the Capitol Police (USCP),

---

*. Their primary protectees are the Senate majority and minority leaders, the majority and minority whips for both chambers, the Speaker of the House, the House Minority Leader, and the Senate President Pro Tempore.

was on the call. They were the ones who most needed to hear this information. They were also the ones who most needed to read the intelligence assessment I had written about the day. However, the information never got to them because the assessment was never properly disseminated.

Jack Donohue opened the call by offering some broad remarks on what we could potentially expect, and then turned things over to me to brief out the specific intelligence. I went over what was happening at the Ellipse and Freedom Plaza, and the various permitted and unpermitted demonstrations scheduled to occur on Capitol grounds. I also stated explicitly much of what I had said in my January 3 intelligence assessment: that the protesters were desperate, believing the vote in Congress scheduled for later that day would decide the election; that there would be extremist groups present; and that many participants would be armed. I shared these points with little fanfare, thinking my words alone would be enough to spur the Capitol Police leadership to action. They were not. Some months after the insurrection, a sergeant with the Dignitary Protection Division told me they had read my assessment, and the evening before the sixth, had instructed the agents under their command to make sure their wills were in order.[4] This person was listening intently on the call, hoping my assessment had changed. It had not. My talking points from this call appear in the final report of the Select Committee to Investigate the January 6th Attack on the Capitol.[5]

Before things got going in earnest at the Ellipse and Freedom Plaza, I went up to the Capitol Police's Command Center. The room was small and dark, with a chill that gave me goosebumps. All four walls were covered with multiple screens that monitored everything from the local air space to nearly every inch of the Capitol Complex, inside and out, as well as other parts of the city.

The USCP leadership sat on a raised platform in the center of the room, with support staff and other agency representatives sitting on the sides and to the back. (Prior to January 6, IICD did not have a seat in the Command Center.) A tiny kitchen lay off to the side of the front entrance to the room, and a slight scent of coffee permeated the air.

There were only a few people present when I arrived. Yogananda Pittman was sitting just to the right of the center seat on the raised platform. The center seat was reserved for the Chief of Police, but Steven Sund was not there yet. Behind Pittman were officers sitting side-by-side at a longer table, and along the sides of the room were representatives from other agencies—the Supreme Court Police, the Sergeant-at-Arms office, the MPD.

I did a quick scan of the screens and saw an eerie calmness throughout the city. There were no cars on the Fourteenth Street bridges. The main thoroughfare in and out the city was empty. The sidewalks were mostly barren. Aside from the mass of people down by Freedom Plaza and the Ellipse, there was nearly no activity.

A few years prior, I had traveled to Dhaka, Bangladesh. When I arrived in the country, they were having a *hartal*, which is a strike and protest, many of which become violent. All the streets in the city were empty and quiet, an exceptional occurrence for what was at the time the second most densely populated city in the world. Later in the day, things would grow violent. That calm before the storm was what I observed looking at Washington, DC, on the cameras in the Command Center. That was when I picked up the phone and made sure my kids were safe. I had never pulled my children out of school before, and I prayed they'd make it home before the violence began. I was bordering on panic, and not just for my children. No one appeared ready for what was about to happen.

On January 6, 2021, my team was primarily responsible for two things: monitoring the protests and sending out updates to a select internal distribution list, and running background and social media checks on individuals who were stopped for possible illegal or suspicious activity.

As I did not want a repeat of my team's performance during the MAGA I and II rallies, where it took them several hours to provide information about suspects who had been stopped, I had made a concerted effort to improve their skills and to set expectations. The day before, I had had someone provide my team with an overview of how to search social media. That training covered the basics, such as how to conduct Boolean searches, how to check internet archives and how to link social media profiles. I also explained to the team that I expected returns on inquiries to occur in a timelier fashion than they had during the first two rallies.

By the morning of the sixth, there were already several people who had been stopped, keeping the agents in the field busy. One of the stops involved a Russian man who claimed to be a journalist. That, in and of itself, wasn't suspicious, but when I was sent a photo of the person's identification, a picture of his visa, it raised major red flags. Since I had worked for immigration before coming to the Capitol Police, I had learned that you could tell a lot from a person's visa. I knew, for example, that this individual was lying. His visa was an "R" visa, which meant he was supposed to be a temporary religious worker in the United States. Journalists don't come to this country on "R" visas. Already, his story didn't match the documents he had presented to the agents. This was something that most at the Capitol Police—or those unfamiliar with immigration law—wouldn't have picked up on.

I quickly expressed my concerns to the leadership of the Investigations Division. This was something that had to be investigated immediately, I told them, when the person was still in front of the agents. There could have been a legitimate reason for the man not to be forthcoming, but there also could be more devious intentions. The Capitol Police never found out because they never asked, and never investigated. After the sixth, I reported this incident to the appropriate agencies and sent them pictures of the documents. They were interested, very much so.

This person wasn't the only Russian with questionable intent to be encountered that day. At around the same time agents were talking to the Russian "journalist," two other Russians were discovered taking pictures of the Capitol from the rooftop of a nearby hotel. They were questioned and asked to stop taking photographs, but no further action was taken beyond my team doing a quick online check on them.

These three incidents occurred in a short span of time. All were potentially serious. Yet it seemed as if the Capitol Police were unable to recognize the larger implications they represented. These, and many other blind spots, caused them to miss an opportunity to potentially change the course of history.

At 1:03 PM, the Capitol Police arrested a man named Lonnie Leroy Coffman. In the back of his pickup truck, they found a cooler containing eleven Molotov cocktails. In addition to being filled with gasoline, the bombs also contained Styrofoam, which was included so that when the device was lit and hit a person, the Styrofoam would melt, adhering to the skin. Thus, the explosives were designed not just to burn, but to maim.

Coffman had driven from his home in Alabama to

Washington, lived in his truck for a week, and then went to Capitol Hill on January 6 with those devices, as well as two unregistered firearms, machetes, a crossbow, and ammunition, intent on battle. Coffman later told a judge at a plea hearing that he "did not plan any action with those things," referencing the Molotov cocktails.[6] For someone who "did not plan any action," he certainly invested much time in preparing. He had gathered up mason jars, drilled a hole into the top of each one of them, filled them with gasoline and Styrofoam, put them in a cooler, loaded the cooler onto his truck, and then driven twelve hours from Falkville, Alabama. In 2022, Coffman was sentenced to forty-six months in prison for his actions on the sixth.

At nearly the same time as Coffman's arrest, two improvised explosive devices were found, one at the Republican National Committee Headquarters at 12:44 PM, and another at the Democratic National Committee Headquarters at 1:07 PM. While the DNC is in a relatively quiet section of the city, the RNC is in a more traveled area located directly across the street from a metro station and the Capitol. It was bold to have placed explosives there, and it was astonishing that they had somehow gone undiscovered between the time they were placed and the next morning when they were discovered.[7]

The news was no better at Freedom Plaza and the Ellipse. The United States Park Police reported that many unattended bags had been left outside the Ellipse. Participants wanting to hear Trump's speech had to be screened in order to get into the area, as is standard for any event where the president will be in attendance. The unattended bags therefore likely contained items that wouldn't make it through security. I reported this troubling information to my leadership. They were warned.

The Capitol Police have an exceptionally high tolerance for those who assert their rights under the First Amendment. Unfortunately, that may have been part of the problem on January 6—the decision makers at the Capitol Police were complacent in thinking this rally would be just like any other.

In the wake of the Challenger space shuttle disaster in 1986, many books came out examining the failures that had led to that moment. But it was the books that examined the culture and leadership failures and their contributions to the explosion that resonated most with me. The O-rings on the space shuttle experiencing a catastrophic malfunction had been the specific reason the shuttle had burst into flames. That is akin to saying that January 6 happened because the Capitol Police were outnumbered by the protesters. But at a deeper level, it was a combination of arrogance, congressional pressure, a comfort with mediocrity and a lack of communication within the Capitol Police that truly caused the calamity, similar to what had happened at NASA several decades earlier.

For example, Capitol Police Chief Steven Sund did not formally request the presence of the National Guard prior to the onset of the riot.[8] And even he had, the Guard did not normally provide protective services at demonstrations or rallies. The last time the Guard had provided protective services at the Capitol was after September 11. Its role is usually limited to helping with road closures and related actions, not riot prevention and control.

In addition, the Capitol Police are a member of the Metropolitan Washington Council of Governments (COG) and could have requested assistance from the multiple jurisdictions that are part of the COG. It did not. Sund also failed to request assistance from other police departments ahead of January 6, and he also failed to cancel leave for Capitol Police officers resulting in only 65 percent of the workforce being on duty during the insurrection.[9]

In my office, I was watching everything that was happening outside the Capitol building in real time, while simultaneously listening to the police radio, feeling a sense of horror as the radio calls went from routine reports, to panic in the officers' voices, to screams.

"We have hundreds of thousands of people here," Trump said, opening his speech at the Ellipse with typical hyperbole.

The west side of the Capitol, which overlooks the National Mall, was covered in scaffolding. The inauguration was only fourteen days away, so workers had been busy assembling the stage for the event. But this platform, with metal rods holding everything together, gave the insurrectionists something to climb on, providing them with a height advantage over the officers. It also provided them with weapons.

"All of us here today do not want to see our election victory stolen by emboldened radical-left Democrats, which is what they're doing . . . We will never give up, we will never concede," Trump continued.

This west side was where most of the insurrectionists would first direct their ire as they walked from the Ellipse and Freedom Plaza up to the Capitol. I didn't know it then as I was not involved in the operational planning, but the west side had less officer coverage from a square footage perspective than the east. But the west would have been the logical place to put more officers because the protesters would be approaching from the National Mall. (Even with more coverage, the east side would be breached as well).

"This the most corrupt election in the history, maybe of the world . . . Today is not the end, it's just the beginning." The crowd at the Ellipse erupted into cheers at Trump's words. To steal a line from *Star Wars*: "So this is how liberty dies. With thunderous applause."

It was like watching a movie, but it was real. And it was happening just outside the building where I was located. I sat at my desk, trying to keep my little piece of the world under control when the world outside was disintegrating into anarchy.

"So we're going to, we're going to walk down Pennsylvania

Avenue ... And we're going to the Capitol ..."

The scene unfolding before me was heartbreaking on many levels. Not only was there the pain of seeing my colleagues being attacked with vicious animosity, but I was also watching an exquisite, sacred, grand building being destroyed. What it represented—freedom, democracy, and the center of the most powerful nation in the world—was even grander.

The officers called for backup, but there weren't enough police in the city to hold back the crowds. The insurrectionists were ready for battle. The Capitol Police were not.

The bike racks surrounding the Capitol to try and keep people away from the building were being lifted and thrown at the outnumbered officers. They were no match for the mob.

"We've lost the line!"

I watched as the windows of the Capitol were smashed, and doors were kicked. I was now viewing live-streamed video on social media that was being taken by the insurrectionists themselves. The pictures were unsteady and chaotic, it was sometimes difficult to see what was happening, but it was easy to see the bedlam, the fury, the fighting.

The insurrectionists chanted "USA!" and other patriotic rallying cries. They also made statements against members of Congress, Vice President Pence, and others that were spit out of their mouths with a ferociousness that represented a clear lust for blood.

When it was clear the Capitol had been breached, Steven Sund left the Command Center and retreated to his office. Chad Thomas, the Assistant Chief for Uniformed Operations, also left. The Capitol was defeated and so, it seemed, were they. But the officers under their command kept battling. They had no choice. They couldn't go into an office and close the door on the whole situation. It was fight or die for the officers. All of them fought. Some of them died.

Amid the chaos, I heard on the radio that shots had been fired. This was both shocking and not surprising at all. My first inclination was to assume it had been one of the protesters who had done the shooting. After all, there were ample amounts of raw intelligence indicating that people would be coming to the rally armed. In my mind, it was just a matter of time until someone was shot. However, it was actually one of the insurrectionists who had been shot by a Capitol Police officer.

Ashli Babbitt was taken into a tunnel under one of the office buildings. The officers attending to her were pleading with the dispatcher to send medical help.

"Where's that ambulance?! She's not doing well," they shouted over the radio.

Dispatch responded that the ambulance was en route but was delayed due to the crowds.

Babbitt would later die at the hospital. I've seen the stories in certain media outlets saying that she was pleading with the police to "call for backup" during the riot.[10] In the videos of

Babbitt in the moments before she was shot, she is seen yelling at the police. Standing to the side of Babbitt, against the wall, is a man with dark hair and a beard, wearing a black face mask. This person worked for the House Sergeant-at-Arms, and I worked with him regularly during my time with the Capitol Police. I asked him if Babbitt really was asking for the police to call for backup. His only response was, "She was on fire."

Ashli Babbitt was killed because she behaved in a way that resulted in her death. Climbing through that window was a suicide mission. Lieutenant Michael Byrd, the officer who shot her, did so because there were members of Congress standing behind him who were in imminent danger. Had Babbitt not been shot and the hallway she was trying to enter been breached, there is little doubt that January 6, 2021, would have ended even worse than it did.

Ashli Babbitt wasn't the only insurrectionist to die on January 6. Kevin Greeson, who had been an avid union man and Obama supporter, switched sides when Trump came to power. According to media reports, he liked Trump because of his background in business.[11] Greeson died of a heart attack that day. Benjamin Phillips also died in a similar manner.[12]

And then there was Rosanne Boyland, who, like Babbitt, has received much attention as a *cause célèbre* from the far right. It was initially reported that she had died after being trampled during the insurrection. While that part is true, the reason she was on the ground in the first place was because she had succumbed to a drug overdose. However, the story the far right has latched onto was that the Capitol Police killed Boyland, kicking and hitting her until she died. They claim that Boyland couldn't have died of a drug overdose because she wasn't a drug user, and that she only had Adderall, an anti-depressant, and caffeine in her blood when she died.** But that isn't true. The DC medical examiner determined that her death was the result of an amphetamine overdose.[13] She was also a convicted felon for a drug-related offense and had a long history of drug abuse.[14] *Vanity Fair,* in a profile about Boyland, highlighted "the sometimes perilous pathway that vulnerable individuals can take when they wholly embrace extremist views, losing rational perspective, alienating loved ones, and putting false hope in conspiracy theories."[15] This description sadly reflects many of

---

**. The conspiracy theories surrounding Boyland's death have largely been promoted by Cara Castronuova. She was a professional boxer and a trainer on the television show *The Biggest Loser.* After January 6, she appeared on far-right podcasts and YouTube channels. She also started Citizens Against Political Persecution, which claims to be a "non-partisan alliance of Americans." However, the organization has almost exclusively focused on advocating for those arrested for participation in the insurrection. In a podcast she did in November 2021 with the far-right group Look Ahead America, a group dedicated to getting "justice" for the January 6 arrestees and promoting election fraud conspiracies, Castronuova explained that Boyland "didn't die of a drug overdose." She also complained that the Department of Justice was trying to "incriminate Trump supporters."

the people present on January 6, not just Rosanne Boyland.

Those who were supposed to be supplying information to the officers over the radio were now silent. At the House Appropriations Committee hearing a month later, Representative Jaime Herrera Beutler asked Yogananda Pittman pointedly, "I want to know why yourself and the other leaders did not maintain or regain control of the comms system because you had a bird's eye view advantage . . . part of the problem there was chaos was because each of these, each, and every one of the officers, boots on the ground commander or not, had to make a decision with no information. Like there was no incoming help as far as they knew. They had no idea what you guys were doing."[16] She chastised Pittman for a lack of "direction and leadership."

The person in charge, Steven Sund, received a phone call from then-Vice President Pence on January 6, just as he relayed in his book. But there was more to the story. Soon after the call, Sund made his way to the Capitol via the underground tunnels which largely remained secure, and met with Pence, who had been hurried away from the House chamber. There, while officers on the floors above and outside the building were fighting for their lives, with not a word of instruction on how they should go about regaining control of the situation, Sund took a picture with the vice president.

From what was conveyed to me by Pittman, Washington, DC Mayor Muriel Bowser stepped in, commanding MPD

Assistant Chief Jeffery Carroll to go to Capitol Police Headquarters to try and regain control of the Capitol.[17] Bowser confirmed sending a commander to the Capitol Police Headquarters in her testimony to the House Select Committee to Investigate the January 6th Attack on the Capitol.[18] MPD Chief Robert Contee also confirmed it was Carroll.[19]

Carroll was a no-nonsense, street savvy cop. He shot from the hip, and took his job very seriously, as he should. It was largely Carroll and Pittman who coordinated the aid that eventually came to the Capitol—677 federal officers and agents and 1,398 officers from state and local police departments.[20] In her testimony to the House Select Committee, Pittman talked about having to make operational decisions outside of her normal authority because "some people were not making decisions."[21]

During all of this, I still had a team to lead. Of the twelve members of the team, myself included, only three were in the office that day, as we were mostly still teleworking due to the pandemic. I had two analysts manning the Sensitive Compartmented Information Facility (SCIF). A SCIF is a secure facility where you can store and view classified material. I gave instructions to the team to screenshot any illegal activity they saw on the videos of the riot they were watching. We took our screenshots and placed them in a folder on the shared drive on our computers. We ultimately amassed hundreds of pieces of data. These would prove to be useful to the investigators in the days following the insurrection.

Hours later, with Congress now evacuated and the insurrection over, I sat in my office, not sure of what to do next. I got up to stretch my legs and take a breather. The normally quiet office was filled with agents waiting to speak to representatives from the Office of Professional Responsibility and others who were already investigating what had transpired. By this time, someone had delivered sandwiches, all different types, turkey, pastrami, roast beef, ham, with all the fixings. They looked delicious but, full of sadness and disappointment, I didn't take one for myself. Instead, I started passing them out to the agents and officers who were standing around, looking shocked and helpless. They stood in silence, eating.

We can measure the effects of January 6 in terms of how many windows and doors were broken, the damage to walls and floors and paintings, how long it took to clean up the Capitol, even in lives lost. But we cannot quantify the cost the attack exacted on our country. There was a loss of confidence in our government, our leadership, and our governing bodies. We had lost our way as a nation.

I don't remember anything after getting home that night. I don't recall eating or showering or going to bed. I know from reviewing my emails some months later, something I've had to do many times since January 6 as I've explained my story to committees and oversight authorities, that I sent messages for a while longer. I also started sending messages again in the very early hours of January 7, so I guess I didn't sleep much that night.

At the time, I thought January 6 was a sprint. Turns out it was a marathon.

EIGHT

Seditious Conspiracies

Sitting in my office on January 6, after quiet had settled upon the Capitol and before Congress returned to complete the certification of the election results, I thought a lot about how something like this could have happened. Not just the physical and logistical elements of the disaster, but what allowed thousands of people to think that an insurrection was acceptable.

The concept of a mob or herd mindset was the subject of many articles in the days and weeks following January 6. *Psychology Today* broke down the behavior of the insurrectionists into six components: deindividuation, which represents a loss of self-awareness; a loss of individual identity; heightened emotions that included excitement and anger; acceptability, which is when normally unacceptable behavior becomes acceptable when committed in a group setting; anonymity; and a diffusion of responsibility.[1]

All these traits were on display on January 6. The first two behaviors on the list, deindividuation and identity, can be seen particularly in the context of QAnon and conspiracy theories. You see the loss of self-awareness and individual identity on right-wing sites like BitChute. To me, it was that loss of individuality that created the absence of self-awareness among the insurrectionists. Many of the theories touted by QAnon, for example, are far removed from reality. Individually, I had hoped in the days preceding that insurrection that most people wouldn't believe the conspiracies that were being discussed online. Unfortunately, once they were together in groups, with everyone talking about and saying the same things, these conspiracies become plausible in the minds of the participants. Combining this with a desire for community and a feeling of belonging made individuality less important.

Much of this had do with the pandemic, which created the perfect storm for something like January 6—not just the loss of jobs and livelihoods that many experienced, but also the social isolation. Trapped in their homes, many people were only interacting with others online, which can lead to self-affirming behavior, especially if others are agreeing with what you were saying. When people feel vulnerable, as many were during the COVID-19 lockdowns, they want to understand why they feel that way. They also want to place blame somewhere, to help them overcome their sense of helplessness. Conspiracy theories helped fill that void.

More than just a mob storming the Capitol, there was in fact a coordinated, preplanned effort on January 6 to forcibly destroy the government of the United States, to oppose the authority of Congress, and to prevent, hinder, and delay the certification of the presidential election results. This is what is known as a seditious conspiracy.*,2

Before January 6, the charge of seditious conspiracy was mostly associated with the Civil War. The law was passed after the war in order to arrest Southerners who potentially wanted to keep fighting against the government. Postbellum, the charge was rarely leveraged. The last time the charge was brought was against members of a militant Christian group in Michigan in 2010, though the charge was later dismissed.[3] The last person to be convicted in the United States of seditious conspiracy before January 6 was Sheik Omar Abdel-Rahman, the mastermind behind the first World Trade Center bombing in 1993.[4]

Given its infrequent use in modern history, having eighteen people charged with seditious conspiracy in the wake of January 6 is remarkable. It was the leaders and members of the Oath

---

*. Seditious conspiracy differs from treason in that it is inciting a rebellion against the government, whereas treason is reserved for those engage in war against the government. It is a precursor to treason. As with any conspiracy, it must require at least two people plotting together for unlawful or harmful purposes. On January 6, the government contended that at least eighteen individuals conspired together to destroy the world's most powerful democracy.

Keepers and Proud Boys who were charged. On its face, it seems to make sense that both groups would band together for a common cause. While they both did heed Trump's call to rebellion, ideologically and organizationally, the two groups were dissimilar, and its leaders did not care much for one other.

The Proud Boys had a more formal structure, with Enrique Tarrio at the top, an executive team known as the "elders" under him, with local and ad-hoc chapters beneath them. The Proud Boys were selective about who could become a member; most members were under the age of thirty. The organizational structure of the Oath Keepers was a lot looser, and they welcomed anyone who paid dues, with few restrictions. Their membership also trended older.

In testimony to the Select Committee to Investigate the January 6th Attack on the United States Capitol, the leaders of the two groups—Tarrio and Stewart Rhodes—gave differing accounts as to why they did not generally coordinate. Tarrio claimed that the Oath Keepers had agreed to provide transportation to the "End Domestic Terrorism" rally in Portland, Oregon, in 2019, but that the group failed to follow through, leaving approximately thirty Proud Boys stranded.[5] For Rhodes's part, he said the Proud Boys were too closely aligned with white supremacists and that he wanted to distance his group from that ideology.[6]

On the evening of January 5, 2021, Tarrio met with Rhodes and others in a parking garage near the Phoenix

Park Hotel.[**] Tarrio had just been released from jail; he had been arrested the day before in connection with his actions at the second MAGA rally on December 12, 2020. It was an apparent coincidence that Tarrio and Rhodes met. Upon his release from jail, Tarrio went to the hotel to pick up his belongings and to touch base with Bianca Garcia, president of the group Latinos for Trump.[7] (Tarrio at the time was serving as the Florida director for the group.[8]) Rhodes was also outside the hotel. The Oath Keepers' attorney, Kellye SoRelle, who was also present, suggested to Garcia that Tarrio and Rhodes meet. The meeting took place a few minutes later.[9] Part of this encounter was caught on video.[10]

When asked about the meeting, Tarrio told the Select Committee that "I just shook his hand, and I said hello."[11] He did not provide additional details about the conversation, or about the video, which shows the two speaking for longer than the amount of time it would take for a simple greeting. SoRelle, in an interview with *Reuters*, said that part of the discussion pertained to legal representation for Tarrio.[12]

Regardless of the contents of their tête-à-tête, Rhodes and Tarrio and their respective groups had in fact planned for weeks before January 6 to change the outcome of the election. Many of the details of the conspiracy would be recounted in their

---

[**]. The Phoenix Park Hotel is located just a couple blocks away from the Capitol.

subsequent criminal trials.

In anticipation of January 6, the leaders of the Oath Keepers and its members had:

- Coordinated travel to Washington, DC, specifically to stop the certification of the electoral vote.
- Organized teams to acquire firearms and ammunition.
- Recruited members to participate in the conspiracy.
- Organized trainings in paramilitary combat tactics.
- Brought weapons and other equipment to staging areas outside of DC.
- Brought paramilitary gear and supplies to Capitol grounds.
- Used social media, messaging apps, and websites to communicate with co-conspirators.[13]

The Select Committee's report indicated that prior to January 6, Stewart Rhodes had spent $7,000 on night vision equipment, $5,000 on weapons and weapon accessories, $6,000 on an AR-15 and its attachments and another $4,500 on firearm accessories.[14]

The Oath Keepers stashed their weapons at a Comfort Inn in the Ballston neighborhood of Arlington, Virginia, about a fifteen-minute drive from the Capitol. The weapons were captured on hotel security cameras, and their location was discussed by group members on text messages.[15] At the second Oath Keepers seditious conspiracy trial, a member recounted how he was brought under the wing of the group's leadership and blindly followed the plan to breach the Capitol on the sixth. The witness had traveled from his home in Florida to DC, bringing with him armor, long-gun cases and ammunition, which he deposited at the hotel in Arlington. He understood that this equipment would be used by the group's so-called "quick reaction force," to "rapidly transfer firearms and other weapons into Washington, DC, in support of operations aimed at using force to stop the lawful transfer of presidential power."[16] Though members of the Oath Keepers claimed that the quick reaction force was established should there be confrontations with antifa, with antifa largely absent on January 6, that argument didn't hold water.

The Oath Keepers and others believed that Trump would evoke the Insurrection Act, resulting in the mobilization of extra-governmental militias to protect the country.[17] In a text message, Rhodes stated, "Either Trump gets off his ass and uses the Insurrection Act to defeat the Chicom puppet coup or we will have to rise up in insurrection (rebellion) against the ChiCom puppet Biden. Take your pick."[18, ***]

***. "Chicom" is derogatory slang referencing a Chinese communist.

At approximately 1:00 PM on January 6, directed by Rhodes and one of his chief lieutenants, Kelly Meggs, members of the Oath Keepers stood outside of the Capitol building. An hour and a half later, Rhodes called Meggs and soon thereafter the first "stack" pushed through the crowd. Lined up one behind the other, a hand on the back of the person in front of them, the stack weaved up the east steps of the Capitol, forcibly entering the building through broken windows. They carried pepper spray, flagpoles, and improvised devices.[19] Upon entry, the group split into two, with one half heading toward the House chamber and the other toward the Senate. A second stack then headed up the east steps toward the Capitol rotunda.

In all, forty-three members of the Oath Keepers were charged in connection with the attack on the Capitol, with twelve charged with seditious conspiracy. Seven members have been convicted of the charge (six at trial and one pleading guilty):

- **Elmer Stewart Rhodes III.** Founder of the Oath Keepers. He did not enter the Capitol on January 6, but was convicted by jury of seditious conspiracy.
- **Kelly Meggs.** The head of the Oath Keepers' Florida chapter and the leader of the first "stack" that entered the Capitol. He was convicted by jury of seditious conspiracy.

- **William Todd Wilson.** Leader of the Sampson County, North Carolina, Oath Keepers chapter. Pleaded guilty to seditious conspiracy.
- **Edward Vallejo.** Oversaw the quick reaction force at the Comfort Inn in Arlington, Virginia, on January 6. He was convicted by jury of seditious conspiracy.
- **Thomas Caldwell.** Oversaw the quick reaction force. He was found not guilty of seditious conspiracy but was found guilty on other felony charges.
- **Joseph Hackett.** A member of the "stack" formation that entered the Capitol. He was convicted by jury of seditious conspiracy.
- **Kenneth Harrelson.** Organizer with the Florida Oath Keepers chapter and ground team lead for the first "stack." He was found not guilty of seditious conspiracy but was found guilty on other felony charges.
- **Joshua James.** Leader of the second "stack" that entered the Capitol. Pleaded guilty to seditious conspiracy.
- **Roberto Minuta.** Assisted in leading "stack" two into the Capitol. He was convicted by jury of seditious conspiracy.
- **David Moerschel.** Joined the first "stack."

formation. He was convicted by jury of seditious
conspiracy.

- **Brian Ulrich.** Joined the second "stack" formation.
  Pleaded guilty to seditious conspiracy.
- **Jessica Watkins.** Head of the Oklahoma Oath
  Keepers group that traveled to DC for January 6.
  She was found not guilty of seditious conspiracy
  but was found guilty on other felony charges.

The seditious conspiracy case against the Proud Boys rested
on the charges that they:

- Recruited members to participate in the January
  6 rally.
- Used social media, messaging apps, and websites
  to communicate with co-conspirators.
- Brought paramilitary gear and supplies to Capitol
  grounds.
- Engaged in multiple meetings to plan their
  activities for January 6.
- Used handheld radios and other communication
  tools during the insurrection to coordinate; direct,
  organize and lead members on Capitol grounds.
- Dismantled barricades at the Capitol.
- Breached and attempted to take control of the
  Capitol building.

- Destroyed property at the Capitol and used force against law enforcement officers.

Just after the 2020 election, Enrique Tarrio had established a new chapter within the Proud Boys, which he called the "Ministry of Self Defense," also known by its initials MOSD, in a nod to the Israeli intelligence service, Mossad. Its purpose was to prepare to fight on behalf of Trump to overturn the results of the presidential election. The leaders of MOSD would recruit and coordinate the Proud Boys who would ultimately attend the insurrection. And indeed, the Proud Boys would be out in force on January 6, 2021, with six charged with seditious conspiracy and fifty-four others charged with various crimes.

The MOSD leadership consisted of Tarrio, John Charles Stewart, Robert Fussell, Zach Rehl, Asher Meza, and Charles Donohoe. Stewart would not travel to DC on January 6 because he had had surgery days earlier. Fussell was also not present, as he missed his flight. He would later cooperate with authorities, providing information that would lead to Tarrio and Rehl, among others, being charged with seditious conspiracy.[20]

On December 27, 2020, the MOSD leadership started a private, encrypted chat entitled "MOSD Prospect Group." That same day, a crowdfunding campaign was set up to cover some of the costs associated with the group's plans for the sixth. Three days later, the group held a video conference call about their plans for the upcoming rally and certification of the election results.

By January 2, 2021, MOSD leaders had created a new chat thread entitled "MOSD Members Group," which initially had sixty-five members. The Proud Boys planned to attend the rally in two groups—MOSD and everyone else. In this new chat group, Charles Donohoe made sure everyone had a copy of the group's plan of action, titled "1776 Returns." This nine-page document outlined plans to storm the "winter palace" as the Capitol was referred to.

The document contained a map of the Capitol and the surrounding area. On the map, three spots were circled—the Russell and Hart Senate office buildings (the third Senate office building, the Dirksen, is attached to the Hart) on the northeast side of the Capitol, the Supreme Court of the United States, and the three House office buildings. The Proud Boys, or at least the authors of the document, intended to "maintain control" over the buildings. Once in control, they would present a list of demands that included holding a new election on January 20, 2021, where only paper, in-person ballot voting would be allowed. They also threatened Mitch McConnell, Kevin McCarthy, Mike Pence, and Bill Gates in the document and added, "Rand Paul and Ron DeSantis, we the people love you."[21] The Proud Boys and other like-minded groups declared the Capitol and the office buildings on the complex as *their* buildings. They were owned by the people, they rationalized, and therefore they had the right to occupy the buildings and to do whatever they wished when inside.

The "1776 Returns" plan proposed having at least fifty people occupy each building, but these instructions vastly underestimated the size of the buildings. It was also scant on details on how to execute the plan successfully. Nevertheless, on the day of the insurrection, one member posted in one of the chat groups, "It's time for fucking war."

The Proud Boys gathered at the Washington Monument early in the morning, around 6:30. By 10:00 AM, approximately 100 members were marching toward the Capitol. They stopped at Peace Circle, which is located on the west side of the Capitol, at Pennsylvania and First Streets NW, near the Capitol reflecting pool.

At 1:00 PM, a message posted in the chat group said, "Push inside!"

NINE

The Toll Taken

When I first started at the Capitol Police, I said to someone in the House Sergeant-at-Arms office that I was in awe of how savvy and poised everyone around seemed. I, on the other hand, felt like this scrappy girl from Boston.

He responded, "That'll be your biggest asset."

I didn't understand it then, but as the days and weeks and months wore on after January 6, I learned he was right. My determination, candor, and unwillingness to back down when the odds were stacked against me were characteristics necessary to survive on the Hill—as well as the fallout from the insurrection.

I had always wanted to work on Capitol Hill, but expected I would just be some anonymous staffer. I never imagined I would not only hold a high-powered position, but that, for better or for worse, people would know who I was. Things certainly didn't play out the way I had anticipated, but it's an experience I will learn to appreciate. Someday.

The morning of January 7, 2021, began with a meeting in Chief Sean Gallagher's office with the leadership of the Protective Services Bureau. Everyone's eyes were glassed over, a combination of exhaustion and sadness. By then, we all knew that Officer Brian Sicknick had been hospitalized and was not doing well. After fighting the rioters the day before and having been hit with a fire extinguisher and doused with pepper spray, Sicknick returned to his division's office, where he collapsed from a stroke. The news that morning was that his family was contemplating the difficult decision to remove him from life support. He would pass before the day's end.

Officer Sicknick laid in honor at the Capitol on February 3, 2021. We stood in the winter sun, three to four deep for several blocks with law enforcement from other departments, waiting along Constitution Avenue for the hearse carrying his body. The officers were mostly quiet, looking out into the street. We first heard the rumble of the motorcycles leading the procession. As the hearse passed by, I wondered what I could have done differently in the lead up to January 6 to have prevented something like this from happening. Once inside the Capitol, Officer Sicknick's body rested in the dimly lit rotunda, his fellow officers watching over him, their breath visible in the chilled air of the room.

The post-insurrection fallout at the Capitol Police was swift. Some left of their own accord, either because they knew they were going to be fired or because they were disgusted by the whole matter. I was surprised, maybe naïve, by how quickly the finger-pointing and blame started after January 6, and was astonished that many fingers were pointing at me.

There has been much discussion about the intelligence in advance of January 6, with some claiming it to be the worst intelligence failure since September 11, 2001.[1] As with 9/11, there was a large scale breakdown in the sense that the intelligence was provided to those who had the authority to act on it, but, for whatever reasons, did not. To be clear, January 6 was not the result of negligence in collecting or analyzing the relevant information. In fact, there was a steady stream of concerning intelligence that was provided to the Capitol Police leadership from the time the January 6 rally was first announced in mid-December until the day of the insurrection.[*,2,3,4,5,6,7,8,9,10,11,12,13,14,15]

---

*. Examples of intelligence that was provided to Capitol Police leadership ahead of January 6 included: December 22, 2020: A summary of concerning items found on donald.win, 4chan, and Discord that included bringing guns to DC, attempting to "overrun" the police, and arresting senators. December 22, 2020: The Hagmann Report posted a video on Rumble encouraging a coordinated armed conflict on January 6. December 22, 2020: IICD drafted an eight-page report about concerning content on donald.win and included sixty-five pages of screen shots showing threads of discussion where people conversed about bringing weapons and organizing on January

It was also not a lack of communication between IICD and the Capitol Police decision-makers that was responsible for what occurred on January 6. Rather, it was a failure to operationalize the intelligence. This was a shortcoming not of the intelligence professionals, but of then Capitol Police Chief Steven Sund. Ultimately, Sund was responsible for not providing the intelligence to the officers on the ground and for not requesting that other law enforcement agencies like

---

6. December 23, 2020: A SITE Intelligence report that said, "I will be armed and won't fuck around . . ." December 23, 2020: Information about https://wildprotest.com was sent directly to Sund. December 27, 2020: A summary of concerning social media posts that included things such as, "Armed and ready, Mr. President," "Show up with guns and threaten them with death," "No revolution has ever been won without violence," and "Kill the opposition." December 30, 2020: Screenshots from donald.win that said, "Kinda begs the question of why are we even [going to the] whitehouse [sic] when the real shenanigans are at the Capitol building." January 1, 2020: Information about the Proud Boys going incognito and not wearing their usual attire. January 1, 2021: I stated, "Just received from MPD, more chatter about possible violence on the 6th." January 3, 2021: I forwarded an article about white supremacists coming to the rally on January 6. January 4, 2021: MPD shared a tip they received from an individual who said he was on a bus coming from Houston to DC, to attend the January 6 rally and "all whom will be carrying weapons and if any law enforcement attempts to take them away there will be a gun fight." January 4, 2021: Leadership was forwarded a series of screenshots from posts on Parler showing weapons and the words, "We are going to execute the worst of the traitors on the spot . . ." and "January 6th may actually be their last day in office." January 4, 2021: Information about a post on donald.win that people bring sniper rifles to the rally on January 6. January 5, 2021: Information was provided about the Oath Keepers' Quick Reaction Force.

the National Guard be present on January 6. He also failed to ensure that there were comprehensive operational plans in place, and demonstrated a lack of courage under fire when the riot was at its worst and the officers needed his guidance.

It is disingenuous to say that IICD was responsible for the lack of operational plans ahead of January 6 because the reorganization I had implemented hindered the team's ability to collect and analyze the intelligence. It is also false to say that prior to my arrival, the team had always provided intelligence for contentious and high-profile events. In his book, *Courage Under Fire*, Sund writes that:

> During my four years with USCP, we had dealt with several very contentious, high-profile events, including two Supreme Court nominations (Brett Kavanaugh and Amy Comey Barrett), some heated health care and immigration demonstrations, and a presidential impeachment trial. During those events, thousands of people protested, sometimes in several locations at the same time, inside and outside the congressional office buildings . . . The IICD had provided accurate and actionable intelligence regarding these events. But now the IICD was facing an organizational crisis, all while the events of January 6 were fast approaching.[16]

In reality, IICD performed better than it ever would have

under its previous leadership. Even if we had not written an intelligence assessment *at all*, we still provided enough information to the Capitol Police leadership to allow them to prepare appropriately. That they did not was a lapse that largely rested on Sund's shoulders. As philosopher and writer Aldous Huxley said, "Facts do not cease to exist because they are ignored."

About a week after the insurrection, references to the FBI's infamous "Norfolk memo" began to emerge. The short memorandum, dated January 5, 2021, featured the attention-grabbing headline, "Potential for Violence in Washington, D.C. Area in Connection with Planned "StopTheSteal" Protest on 6 January 2021."[17] The memo went on to discuss an online right-wing thread that made "specific calls for violence," adding that people needed to "Be ready to fight. Congress needs to hear glass breaking, doors being kicked in, and blood from their BLM and Pantifa slave soldiers being spilled. Get violent. Stop calling this a march, or rally, or a protest. Go there ready for war. We get our President or we die. NOTHING else will achieve this goal."[18]

The "Norfolk memo" was purported to be the smoking gun that showed that there had been intelligence warnings about what would happen on January 6. While IICD had similar intelligence through other sources noting that the Capitol would be the target, I nonetheless was concerned that I had received the memo and somehow missed it. I furiously went through my emails, my heart racing. During my time at the Capitol Police, it was not unusual to get upward of several hundred emails on a daily basis. I scrolled on and on, looking through multiple folders until I finally found the memo. I had received it . . . on January 6, 2021, at 5:53 PM. After the insurrection was essentially over.

Like wildfire scorching through a forest, whispers swiftly spread through my office. Who had gotten the memo? One lieutenant and a couple of task force agents had indeed received the memo the night before, on January 5. But it was a very busy time, as we were all preparing for the rally the next day, the email came in the evening and was not flagged as being important. There was also no phone call from the FBI alerting the Capitol Police of the intelligence they had received from their Norfolk Field Office. Just one inconspicuous email message, less than twelve hours before the violence would begin.

It also came to light that the intelligence report IICD had sent out for January 6 included a statement that the likelihood of civil disobedience for the events at the Ellipse and Freedom Plaza were "improbable," and that the other events—there were twenty-four possible protests listed in the report— happening on Capitol grounds ranged from "remote" to "highly improbable" to "improbable." The report, which we issued daily, was long, running about fifteen pages each day. It included every demonstration in Washington, DC, that we had a record of, whether it would take place that day or several months later. The report also included information on every congressional hearing taking place, whether relevant to the Capitol Police or not. Because of its length and questionable relevance to day-to-day operations, most people didn't read the report.

When I first arrived at the Capitol Police, I immediately recognized that the report needed a major revamp. In early November 2020, I met with the primary author of the report and mentioned that I thought it was a bit long and asked them to think about how we could redesign it to make it more succinct and useful to readers. In early December, Jack Donohoe provided the author with a sample of the NYPD daily report and said that ours should be something similar. Unfortunately, the report was not revised before January 6.

After the insurrection, the report from January 6, 2021, received a lot of attention, with many pointing to it as *the* intelligence failure.[19] It was a failure, but the weight attributed to it was much more than it deserved. The report was emailed daily to only a handful of people. After the insurrection, the Capitol Police's IT department pulled a list of who had opened the document on January 6, which revealed that only six people had looked at it that day, two of them IICD employees.

Steven Sund likes to hang his hat on this report as the reason he did not plan more effectively ahead of the sixth. In a letter he wrote to then Speaker of the House of Representatives Nancy Pelosi explaining why the Capitol Police were not better prepared on January 6, 2021, he stated, "The IICD Daily Intelligence Report assessed 'the level of probability of acts of civil disobedience/arrests occurring based on current intelligence information,' as 'Remote' to 'Improbable' for all of the groups expected to demonstrate on Wednesday, January 6, 2021."[20] But in writing this, he was being dismissive of all the other intelligence and warnings he received. It was like when I learned I was pregnant soon after having my first baby. I took several pregnancy tests and was in disbelief that they were positive. However, one test was negative, and I joked that at least that one had gotten it right. Despite that one contradictory sign, I was still pregnant.

In spite of the evidence that the blame lay elsewhere, following the insurrection there was an obvious undertone of resentment against me from both the Capitol Police officers and my own division.

In the aftermath of the sixth, I was asked to give intelligence briefings at roll calls. Since most divisions work in three shifts (morning, afternoon, and midnight), I had to do separate briefings for each of them. (I ended up doing twenty-five or so separate briefings.) Most of those I briefed were officers, but I also briefed the Command Center (many employees there are civilians) and the Security Services Bureau (also mostly civilians). In some ways I was being thrown to the wolves. During these briefings, several officers let it be known that they were unhappy with me. To them, I was the face of their frustrations with the entire department.

"We never received your intelligence assessment," one yelled at me. It was true, but prior to January 6, I hadn't been permitted to distribute anything to the entire workforce.

In the dark basement hallway of one of the House office buildings where the officers began their shifts, another officer demanded to know, "Why hasn't the Capitol Police tried to infiltrate the Proud Boys?"

On it went like that. I listened to the officers and took their blows, unflinching. I didn't get flustered and answered their accusations head on, hoping my answers clarified where their discontent should be directed. Anger was rising inside of me, too.

After January 6, all personnel within the Capitol Police were required to work twelve-hour shifts, with no days off—including weekends or leave—permitted until after the inauguration on January 20. At a time when we were emotionally defeated and/ or physically damaged, we had to work harder than ever.

As a single mother to two young daughters, these long shifts were not something I had signed up for. I'd leave for work earlier than I normally would because the sooner I got started, the sooner I could call it a day. I'd return home at my regular time and put my kids to bed and then work another two to three hours to finish up my required twelve hours. It was exhausting. Somehow, I found time to do laundry, putting it in the wash before I went to bed and moving it to the dryer in the morning when I woke up, but I had no energy to fold it. It just piled up on a chair.

The consequences of the emotional anguish in the wake of January 6 were even greater, especially for the officers who had been on the front lines. One Capitol Police officer, Howard Liebengood, committed suicide, as did three Metropolitan Police officers, Jeffrey Smith, Gunther Hashida, and Kyle DeFreytag. The insurrection had not only altered the course of the United States, but had also shattered the lives of many of those who had been there that day, doing their jobs.

The Capitol Police sent out a message to the workforce highlighting the mental health services available to all employees. Supervisors were encouraged to promote these services, so I sent out a message to my team:

It has been a difficult week for all of us. Two of our USCP family members are no longer with us. We are facing scrutiny and pressure and we are all working tirelessly. I commend you for your strength and efforts and know that there is no shame or weakness in asking for help. Quite the contrary, it shows just how strong you are. I would like to highlight the message below and I encourage you to seek help if you need it. Thank you for your commitment to the USCP mission and stay well.[21]

Even though we were all struggling, our work continued. I was asked to ensure that the SCIF, the secure facility where classified material was viewed and stored, remained open during the overnight shift. Though there had been no classified information that had come in warning of the insurrection, the Capitol Police were suddenly concerned they would get such information after the fact.

I reached out to the person who worked the shift, telling them they needed to come into the office the night of the sixth.

"I'm currently sick. Let me know if you still want me in the office," they asked, having missed the entire day.

"Sick with Covid?" I asked.

"Sick with a sore throat. Doctor said to stay home and away from people."[22] I was forced to ask someone who had worked all day to cover the overnight shift as well.

The same person then proceeded to email me the next day, blaming me for the events on the sixth. "Maybe it's time to have another meeting," they wrote. "Working both sides of the coin. This is part of the reason yesterday took place . . . No one, no other agency regardless of who your contacts or friends are, are going to do your job for you."[23]

I could appreciate that this person was having an emotional response. They were rightfully upset, but their anger was misplaced. There would have been no warning about January 6 if I hadn't written one and alerted the Capitol Police leadership.

This person drafted an even angrier message a few days later, which ended with, "my blood will be on your hands."[24]

Blood on my hands? Though this person was prone to hyperbole, I did take what they were saying seriously. My immediate thought was that they were suicidal. This didn't seem a stretch given their previous outbursts, and the fact that another officer had just committed suicide.

I didn't see the message until Jack Donohue called to tell me about it. "I'll handle it," I told Jack, though I was not happy that his first inclination was to contact me and not take immediate action himself.

I got in touch with Sean Gallagher's executive officer and told them I had concerns that the employee was suicidal. They, in turn, contacted internal affairs, which quickly dispatched someone to this person's home and seized their service weapon and required that they contact the Employee Assistance Program. The person was later placed on administrative leave.

I thought I had handled the situation well, given the circumstances. Kimberley Schneider, the new acting head of the Protective Services Bureau (PSB), had a different opinion.

She had assumed the PSB commander role after Steven Sund resigned and Yogananda Pittman became the acting Chief of Police, with Sean Gallagher filling Pittman's previous position as Assistant Chief. Schneider told Jack and I that she wanted to meet with us separately.

I met with her first. Her office was on the west side of the building, overlooking Upper Senate Park. In the distance, I could see the Washington Monument. On one of her walls hung a photograph of the Twin Towers, an ode to Schneider's New York upbringing, though she had no discernible accent. She kept the doors to the cabinets above the side of her desk open, lining them with flowers and trinkets. In the corner of her office was an incense diffuser, which billowed with the scent of lavender. Long vines of a plant poured over the sides of a file cabinet, and on the floor against the wall were large butterfly wings cut from cardboard. They were remnants of a protest; written across the wings was the word "dreamer."

"I'm only going to have this conversation with you once," she started. In front of her on her desk was a small, purple notepad filled with talking points for the meeting. "The way you handled last night was disgraceful."

Disgraceful?

"I hear what people are saying around here," Schneider continued. "I talk to the people on your team. They find you cold and tyrannical and they don't like working in IICD. Some of them have asked to transfer out."

It wasn't news to me that some of the members of my team were not happy. It was obvious from their behavior, and their frequent resistance to the changes I was trying to make. But the way Schneider was telling me this wasn't constructive. It also wasn't lost on me that someone telling you that you're perceived as "cold and tyrannical" could come across as . . . cold and tyrannical.

"You set the standards too high for the team," she added.

The standards had to be set high because the stakes were even higher, especially now. I was trying to professionalize the team and bring them up to the level of other intelligence agencies in the federal government. It was something that absolutely had to be done.

"I'm not telling you how to run your team, but you're giving the analysts different responsibilities and then get upset when they can't do the work . . ."

"I'm trying to make the team more efficient . . . ," I interjected.

"I'm still speaking," she snapped. "They haven't had any training. If I put you out on the street with an MP7 without any training, you wouldn't know what to do."

I wanted to say that that may have been the case on day one, but if I were out on the street every day for fifteen years— the amount of time many of the analysts had been in their positions—I would have figured out what to do. If I didn't get formal training, I would have taken the initiative and sought it out on my own. It was a matter of self-motivation and professional responsibility. I'd ask questions, I'd obtain expertise from those who did know what they were doing. After fifteen years, I'd be an expert. But I didn't say any of this to Schneider.

"You need to go back to the way Norm did things." She was referring to Norm Grahe, Jack's predecessor. However, we were in this situation because of the way Norm had run the team, I thought to myself. It was his inability to provide training, and to hold the employees accountable for their performance, as well as his failure to work with others both inside and outside of the Capitol Police that had contributed to the team's dismal performance. He had also shown little interest in showing me the ropes when I came on board. Even if I wanted to return to the way Norm did things, I wasn't sure what that would entail.

Schneider also told me that the message I had sent to the team the day before about reaching out for counseling if they needed it was "offensive" and that it "fell flat" because I wasn't a cop. Schneider was about the same age as me and had worked at the Capitol Police her whole career. Her perspective was narrow, and she didn't appreciate that most of the recipients of my message were civilians. Even though I was not a cop, I could still understand what hurt felt like. She again said I was "disgraceful," this time in the context of the counseling message.

The meeting went on for a while, with Schneider giving me a laundry list of reasons why I was a horrible leader and an awful person and why the team was justified in their hatred of me.

I returned to my office and immediately wrote a memo to myself, documenting the conversation I had just had. I was scared. It was apparent Schneider didn't like me and as a probationary employee, she had the power to fire me without cause. I had thought that something like that couldn't happen because I was the one who had been working tirelessly to improve the team and had warned of the impending doom on the sixth. Schneider didn't see it that way and had made it clear she would fight against the changes I was trying to make to the Capitol Police's intelligence division. I was sounding the alarm in a place that didn't want to hear it.

I sat in my office the remainder of my shift, wondering what I could do to protect myself. My first inclination was to start looking for a new job, but I didn't. Instead, I became resolute in my determination to make the situation better. Not better in terms of improving the way Schneider and some on the team viewed me, but in making the necessary changes so that something like January 6 would never happen again. I wouldn't leave until the Capitol Police had a viable intelligence division, capable of collecting and analyzing intelligence important to the department's mission. I had a duty to my country to do that, despite the challenges before me.

When I returned home that night, I reached out to Brian Murphy. He was the individual who had written intelligence reports warning of Russia's efforts to interfere with the 2016 election—intelligence that Trump mandated he change.[25] Brian refused and sought whistleblower protection. I had spoken with him a few times when I was at DHS, and he was the only person I could think of who would even have a remote idea of what I was going through. I sent him a text on LinkedIn, and he immediately called me.

"I'm going to connect you to my attorney," he said. "Once you have an attorney, you'll feel so much better." He explained what would happen next and gave me the guidance and support I needed. I am forever grateful and indebted to him for that conversation.

Within minutes, I was speaking with Mark Zaid, a well-known attorney specializing in whistleblower protections and other high-profile areas of law. He sued the country of Libya after the bombing of Pan Am Flight 103 and won. He had also sued Trump, which prompted his first impeachment trial. And now he was my lawyer. It was at this point that I thought I was in real trouble if an attorney of Zaid's stature would take my case. It was one thing to be a spectator watching a Washington scandal unfold. It was another thing altogether to be part of one. It was a place I didn't want to be.

"You doing okay?" the sergeant who sat outside my office asked me when I came into work the next morning. It was something he asked me often, but today that was all it took to open the floodgates. I cried at his desk, telling him what had transpired in my world over the past few days. He listened without judgment.

In the days following the sixth, many would come to me for comfort and reassurance. In one such instance, a different sergeant came into my office and sat in front of me. He was someone I saw every day, but our conversations didn't usually go beyond the usual greetings. He sat quietly at first. I met him with a smile.

He inhaled deeply. "I made an appointment with EAP. I know I need to talk to someone, but I don't know what I'm going to say." I thought this man, with his commanding presence, who was charged with protecting others, might cry in front of me. I would have sobbed with him if he had.

"You don't need to say anything if you don't want," I told him. "They're there to support you and to listen. Sometimes just knowing someone is there is helpful."

I thought it was odd that this man, strong and masculine, would open up to me. I never thought of myself as someone who came across as approachable or warm. This was also coming on the heels of being told I was "cold and tyrannical." Maybe he felt he could come to me because I was one of the only women in the office. Maybe it was because I had an office with a door that closed. Maybe it was because I worked in intelligence and by virtue of my position, was privy to lots of secrets, and I could keep them, and his. Whatever the case, I was happy to listen.

A few months after January 6, I had to call the United States Citizenship and Immigration Services (USCIS) district director in Boston. He was an older gentleman and the person who had first hired me to work in government. Whenever I made it back to Boston, I would stop by and see him, and our conversations always started with him asking about my family and how I was doing personally. He had been disappointed when I left USCIS because he thought I would take over for him when he retired.

On the call, we exchanged the usual civilities, and he asked, as usual, how I was doing.

"It's been hard," I answered honestly.

With typical wisdom, he replied, "You know, Julie, sometimes we're put in places, and we don't know why we're there, but we should trust we are put there for a reason." I guess I hadn't thought of it like that, though I still wasn't sure why I had ended up where I did. Maybe that answer will come to me somewhere down the road.

When I worked at USCIS, I had overseen the implementation of the flurry of executive orders Trump had issued in the first few months of his presidency, many of them restricting lawful immigration. They were wildly unpopular in an agency whose mission was to welcome immigrants to this country. While the orders were coming from Trump, it was my job to see them to fruition. The ire the agency employees felt toward the then president was largely taken out on me. I was a civil servant and unless the orders were illegal, I had to do my job, regardless of my personal feelings. There were many moments when I broke down in tears. At the time, I thought that would be the biggest challenge I'd face in my career. Instead, it gave me the emotional resilience I needed to face an even greater one.

TEN

High Stakes

The inauguration of President Biden came and went uneventfully, which was a relief to the Capitol Police. They badly needed a "win."

The days leading up to the ceremony had been filled with a mixture of apprehension and scrutiny. With a fence around the Capitol, and the National Guard and law enforcement from around the country present, DC looked like a war zone. The Capitol Complex was desolate aside from police officers and the military. My office was within the fenced-in area; I had to pass through three checkpoints to get inside. The streets around the Capitol were also closed. One afternoon I had to get my second Covid vaccine at the health center in the Longworth House Office Building. I was able to walk there right in the middle of the street, past the Supreme Court, because there were no cars on the road.

After the inauguration, I needed to adjust the schedules of my team members in order to provide adequate coverage in the SCIF. Most of the team was still teleworking due to the pandemic, but those manning the SCIF needed to be in the office, as classified materials cannot be taken offsite. Everyone's hours remained the same, but due to some employees finally having time off, I sometimes needed to switch the days analysts came into the office. I asked one analyst to come in on one of their usual telework days. They did not take well to the request and reported it to Kimberly Schneider. After some back and forth, Schneider sent a message to Jack Donohue, "Is Julie having a problem assigning work or something?"[1]

I wasn't having "a problem assigning work." If Schneider understood what was going on with my team, she would have known why I was asking this employee to come in. It was frustrating fighting all the time to get certain team members to do their job and even more frustrating not having the support and backing of my superiors. I was simultaneously being told by the USCP leadership, congressional oversight committees, and the media that the intelligence division needed to be reformed, while also having people within the Capitol Police doing everything they could to ensure that those reforms would never happen.

In September 2021, four analysts within IICD claimed whistleblower protection. The timing of this correlated with me putting the finishing touches on their terminations. I had spent nearly a year documenting their performance and conduct issues—this was how long it took to fire someone in the federal government. Their whistleblower claim was based on the false accusation that they had provided intelligence to me ahead of January 6 and that I had ignored it. They also claimed that my efforts to merge the two teams within my division—the Open-Source Section and the Intelligence Analysis Section—caused confusion resulting in the supposed intelligence failures on January 6.[2]

The main problem was that these team members lacked basic analytical skills. For example, prior to January 6, I had tasked two of the analysts with writing an information paper about assassinations and attempted assassinations of elected officials. My thought process was that, if done correctly, this information could provide insight into the motivations and warning signs of potential assassins. The analysts provided what I had asked, but without any kind of analysis. What they gave me was a multi-page paper that listed many assassinations and attempted assassinations, but little more. This would have been fine for a first draft, but not a supposed final report.

I also received multiple emails from the two analysts saying that they were not able to conduct open-source research (i.e., unclassified, public), as it wasn't their area of expertise.[*]

---

[*]. Repeatedly, IICD intelligence analysts who had been on the team for more than a decade stated they were unable to conduct basic open-source research, though nearly all the intelligence work IICD

[3, 4, 5, 6, 7, 8, 9, 10, 11] This meant that they had been unable to collect intelligence ahead of January 6, as nearly all it had come from open sources.

After they had been terminated, the analysts went to the media with a litany of complaints against me. One article published by CNN stated that, "In December, [Farnam] asked a couple members of the team for an historical overview of assassination attempts both in the US and abroad, including 'all levels of the government worldwide.'" The article added a quote from one of the disgruntled former employees, "I really don't know the purpose of an assignment like that . . . I don't think that's a good use of resources."[12] The GOP "shadow committee" for January 6 also asked me about this, as they had previously spoken to the terminated employees. I told them diplomatically that I gave the analysts assignments that allowed them to

---

completed used open-source material. These same analysts would go on to claim before the GOP Shadow Committee that they "at the time of January 6, we were not doing proactive searches of social media like we had been before," though written evidence establishes that they, by their own admissions, lacked the skills necessary to collect the relevant intelligence. The analysts stated, "I was only able to conduct a limited search of social media," "I'm not experienced in social media," "I need your guidance/direction as my inexperience [sic] at this critical time," "can someone kindly advise me as to who are our partners," "I can't speak to any standard if you're referring to [social media] because several of us were never trained in that particular area," "is there specific verbiage to determine if it's a threat," and "I didn't take any of the OSINT classes, [sic] prior to January because it wasn't an area that I specialized on in the past."

"positively contribute to the mission of the team."[13]

In another instance, I proposed switching one of the whistleblowers to the evening shift because the team was lacking in coverage during that time. I gave both Sean Gallagher and Kimberly Schneider the heads up about this, and I also provided the analyst with fifteen-days' notice before the change became effective. While I understood that alterations to a work schedule can be disruptive, we were a small team, which necessitated the need for some flexibility. This person was also the most junior member of the team.

I expected the analyst to put up a fight, as they had done with nearly everything I proposed or requested of them. However, rather than responding to me directly, the analyst drafted a lengthy email to Schneider, including one paragraph dedicated to how the schedule change would impact their dog walker.[14] Their argument also centered around the erroneous belief that they were not the most junior member of the team.

I went directly to Kimberly Schneider after reading the email. "I saw the email about the schedule change," I said to her. "It's a dog. I have a dog and somehow, I am able to find a dog walker despite all the hours I work. I can also attest to the fact that finding childcare is even harder and still I manage to get that done, too. I need this person to work evenings because we have work to do and not enough people covering evenings. When I bring new people onboard, we can see about changing their schedule to working mornings."

Schneider didn't say anything in response. She just stood there, silent. However, within a few days, the analyst submitted a request for a reasonable accommodation stating that they had a medical condition that required them to work the morning shift. The request was granted. When the Office of the General Counsel of the Capitol Police learned of the accommodation after the analyst had been notified they were going to be terminated, they were none too happy the request had been granted in the first place.[15]

Throughout the remainder of the winter and into the spring and summer of 2021, I quietly began seeing Shane Lamond. For our first date we met at the same place where we had first crossed paths at the holiday party. This was only the second time I had met him in person.

We sat at a small table near the fireplace in the back and ordered beers. He smiled and the way he looked at me, I knew this wasn't a work meeting. I had butterflies in my stomach and struggled to make small talk.

He asked me if I was single. I told him, yes, I was divorced. I noticed the ring on his finger. "Are you married?" I asked.

"I'm working on my second divorce now."

Though he was still married, I accepted his declaration of an impending divorce. In Virginia there is no such thing as a legal separation; you just need to be living apart for six months (without kids) or one year (with kids), with a few exceptions, such as abuse in the relationship. I dated before my divorce was final, so I saw no harm in going out with Shane.

We chatted for over an hour, talking about our kids, work, and what we liked to do when we weren't on the job. By the end of the evening, we had planned to meet up again a few days later.

For our second date, we went to Sonoma Cellars. It was in an old building, a house converted into a restaurant. The courtyard in the back was closed for the winter so we dined upstairs. We sat across from one another, the only two in the drafty room, sharing a bottle of malbec. After dinner we went back to my house, where we spent several hours talking and kissing in my living room.

Over the next few months, we saw each other regularly. I also spoke to him daily at work. I never told Jack or anyone else at my office about our relationship. I'm not sure how Jack would have reacted knowing that he no longer had primacy over all things Shane. The relationship also provided me with insight as to just how much information Jack had withheld from me. Information was the currency of intelligence. But Shane was my secret. The information he provided to me was a bonus, but it was not the reason I continued to see him. Could I have navigated that situation differently? Yes, but the opportunity was there with Shane, and I took it.

I didn't know it then, but Shane was sharing information with others as well. Enrique Tarrio, leader of the Proud Boys, was working as an informant for several police departments, including the Metropolitan Police. Shane was his point person within the department. In our chats about work, Shane would often tell me that he had spoken with Tarrio. I also knew that they texted each other frequently. We didn't go into much detail on what they discussed, but I assumed Shane was trying to gain intelligence about the Proud Boys. Later it would be revealed that Shane was doing more than just gathering information.

Informants have always made me uncomfortable. When I worked for Immigration and Customs Enforcement, I handled payments to some of the office's informants. I recalled my boss telling me how much he hated informants and that they were more trouble than they were worth. He warned me that if during my career I ever had to deal with one, to always keep them at arm's length. I had not forgotten that advice.

Shane didn't talk much about politics, but I knew he was a Republican, though he never openly declared his support for Trump, at least not to me. However, on the bumper of his gray sedan was a sticker of the comic book character, The Punisher. Although the character itself is a crime-fighter, it was a symbol that had been adopted by the far-right. I found it odd that Shane would have this on his vehicle, though I never questioned him about why it was there. Knowing now about his relationship with the Proud Boys and perhaps other extremist groups, the symbol makes more sense.

Several months into our relationship, Shane called me one day, upset. He had been brought into his boss's office and asked to turn over his work phone. He said it had something to do with Tarrio. After some back and forth, Shane revealed that there was a grand jury subpoena for his phone. I wasn't overly concerned, as Tarrio had all sorts of legal troubles. That his communications with his law enforcement handlers were part of an investigation didn't surprise me.

I did, however, recognize that, grand jury secrecy or not, Washington was a small town and gossip traveled fast. That was why conspiracies about the deep state make me laugh because there are no secrets in Washington. That said, I didn't want my bosses at the Capitol Police to catch wind of my relationship with Shane through the DC grapevine. I immediately got in touch with Sean Gallagher and told him about the subpoena and the relationship. I thought that was the end of it. It would be . . . for a few months.

In the meantime, Kimberly Schneider carried on in her quest to bully me into submission. On February 18, 2021, she sent Jack and me a message saying she had set up a meeting for us. No further details were provided. Immediately, I was concerned. I asked for more information about the meeting. She eventually explained that she was going to have us meet with a consultant who would talk to us about how to better communicate with our team. I welcomed opportunities for professional development and had recently completed the Executive Leadership program at American University.

It was immediately clear, however, that Schneider was not following proper government protocols for procuring outside services, as the person she was recruiting to "help" us carried questionable credentials. We believed she was trying to set up a platform to give the underperforming employees on our team the opportunity to express their displeasure with us. There were some on the team who indeed hated us. However, I wasn't going to let my desire to be universally liked get in the way of making hard choices so that the Capitol Police would have a viable intelligence division. The pressure to make those changes was especially high after January 6. Schneider was either ignorant of this fact or was fully aware and chose to put personal relationships ahead of professional responsibilities.

I had experienced these "listening sessions" in the past. If done right, they are immensely helpful. If not, they only serve to leave everyone feeling like they've been attacked, and breed discord and resentment. I didn't have much optimism, given Schneider's handling of the situation with the team already. I told her I'd attend this meeting after consulting with my attorney to see if he could be present. At first, she said she'd check with the consultant to see if they'd be okay with my lawyer attending. However, when the time to meet came, the only ones there were Jack and me. Schneider didn't show, nor did the consultant. She never let us know the meeting had been canceled.

If something good came out of January 6, it was that Congress was ready and willing to provide resources and money to IICD. This would allow us to hire additional staff. The division had posted two job announcements, one for internal candidates and the other for external candidates, before Jack and I came on board. In April 2021, we finally started conducting interviews, using the two vacancy announcements to fill several positions.

Jack and I had differences of opinion as to what type of people we wanted to hire. I was interested in individuals with formal intelligence training, including report writing and analysis. Jack wanted a law enforcement background, despite the fact that many of the underperforming analysts on the team had either been cops prior to moving to intelligence or had worked in other law enforcement capacities. The candidates we ultimately settled on came from a variety of backgrounds, a mix of intelligence community professionals, law enforcement, and others with applicable skills such as investigative journalism.

On the day we had designated for the interviews, things did not go as planned. It was a Friday afternoon. Jack was in New York, and we were holding the interviews virtually. I sat in my office, the door closed, asking the same questions to a series of prospective employees. All was going fine until I started to hear people running around and yelling outside my office. That was unusual, as the office atmosphere was generally low key and quiet.

"Can you hold on for a moment? I think something's going on." I stopped the interview I was doing and poked my head out of my office.

"What's going on?" I asked my executive officer.

"Shots fired." He said nothing else before exiting the office suite.

Soon thereafter, my phone started ringing and then the emails came, and I understood what was going on. Noah Green had rammed his car into a checkpoint at the Capitol. One officer, Billy Evans, had been killed. Another officer, Kenny Shaver, was seriously injured. As in the *Book of Revelations*, a source from which Green drew much inspiration, "And I looked, and behold . . . its rider's name was death."[16] Green exited the car after hitting the officers and lunged at another officer with a knife. That officer shot and killed him.[17]

After the incident, Sean Gallagher asked me to personally research Green and draft an assessment of my findings. I sifted through everything Green had posted online. In researching a person of interest, you must first find their social media profile and confirm their identity. In this case, I knew what Green looked like and his social media contained pictures of him, rendering confirmation easy. Often, individuals use the same social media handles across multiple sites, making it relatively simple to map their online footprint. Once their identity has been confirmed, I start reading, sometimes going back years to see the trajectory of their radicalization.

Initially, Green's social media was full of normal things college-aged boys would post—lots of talking about sports and girls. But as time progressed, posts about basketball drafts were replaced by anti-government rantings from the Nation of Islam and lengthy diatribes about passages from the Bible.

In 2020, Green moved to Botswana. In my experience, this is common with people suffering from mental illness, as there seems to be this pervasive belief that a change of scenery will help them. Sometimes it is the person themselves, recognizing that they are struggling with what is going on in their head, who prompts the move, as was the case with Green. Other times, it is the family who sends the person to a new location hoping they'll get better. In my time before working in the government, I had an adult student from South Korea who was sent by her family to the United States to help "cure" her. She was suffering from severe mental illness and the move did nothing to save her from her own mind.

Even though his family knew he was struggling mentally and worried about him, no assistance came for Noah Green, and in his wake, he left a trail of devastation.

There we stood on the street, again, in silence, the sun beaming down upon us like it had in February, as we waited for Officer Evans's casket to pass. Prior to January 6, the Capitol Police had only lost five officers in the line of duty in its entire history. Since the insurrection, it had lost two officers in action, plus another to suicide. Standing there waiting for another fallen officer was an experience I wished to never experience in my life, yet it was happening for the second time in as many months.

When Jack returned to the office a few days after the Green incident, he was noticeably upset. He would snap when asked a question. In one instance, he received a phone call from a member of the media, something I would come to experience as well, and was livid that they were asking him questions about January 6, yelling after he hung up the phone. Something was up.

When he accepted the position with the Capitol Police, it was with the understanding that he would return to New York on the weekends where his wife remained. After January 6, with all of us working extended hours, his trips to New York became less frequent, which placed a strain on his marriage. The death of yet another officer added to that stress.

One day, while I was talking with Jack in my office, I noticed my Special Security Officer (SSO) walking past several times, like they wanted to talk to me, but didn't want to interrupt the conversation I was having. An SSO oversees the management of the SCIF, among other responsibilities.

My phone rang.

"I need to talk to you right away," the SSO said.

I finished up with Jack. When he left, the SSO entered my office and closed the door. It was never a good sign when an employee walked into your office and closed the door.

"Jack came into the SCIF this morning," the SSO told me.

Jack did not have the security clearance that would permit him to be in the SCIF, but he could go if he signed in, was escorted, and everyone put away their classified materials. He made a habit of going there each morning to say hello to the staff.

"He took the daily read book and started going through it," the SSO shared breathlessly, their voice shaky. "I had to tell him he wasn't cleared to read it and I took it away from him. What should I do?" The daily read book contained a summary of highly classified intelligence for the day.

"Report it as you would any other security violation. I'll deal with the higher ups."

I immediately told Sean Gallagher what had happened. Then I sent Jack an email about what he had done, not because I didn't want to have a difficult conversation with him face to face, but because I wanted to have written documentation about having addressed the issue with him. Accessing classified information without authorization was a serious offense.

Later that morning, Jack stormed into my office. He closed

the door. His head was lowered, not making eye contact with me, but he spoke with force. "Did something happen in the SCIF?"

"Yes, something did." I paused, deciding if I should let him tell me what happened or if I should jump right into the confrontation. Given his question and my response, maybe that train had already left the station. "Did you look at the daily read book?" I continued before he had an opportunity to respond. "You know you don't have the clearance to read that. There is a cover sheet. YOU are the Director of Intelligence. YOU should know better. You're not even supposed to be in the SCIF."

"Oh, so I guess it's all coming crashing down now." His eyes welled up. Jack tended to view the world fatalistically. Except this time, he may have been right.

Within several days of this incident, Jack left the Capitol Police, leaving me to serve as the acting director of IICD, a position I would hold for more than a year.

A few weeks later, Kimberly Schneider and I were invited to a luncheon with other women in government, coordinated by the intel head at Health and Human Services. Both Schneider and I were on the same email chain about the luncheon, and we both had confirmed our participation.

When the time for the lunch came, I was distracted by work and forgot about it, until I received a phone call from someone at another agency asking if I was going. I immediately put aside my work and headed to the restaurant.

When I arrived, there were eight other women there, seated at a long table. All of them already had food in front of them. The woman who had invited me boisterously introduced me to the others. I had not met most of them, but they all greeted me with a smile. All except one.

I took the only seat available at the right-hand end of the table. Schneider was sitting directly across from me. She had been in the office all morning. She'd walked past my office to exit the building to go to the luncheon, never stopping to ask if I was coming or if I wanted to travel together.

This was the last straw for me. I expected more of her as a leader. Later, I sent her a message requesting a meeting, outlining some of the concerns I had with our relationship at work:

> I'd like to meet to see if we can find a way to work together in a more collaborative way. I was really hurt today that you didn't see if I wanted to go over with you to the luncheon and last week when you wanted to call me from your office for a meeting, it was also hurtful . . . The same holds true for the biweekly classified briefing I provided on May 18th. I try to select pieces of intelligence that are pertinent to what we do here at USCP and there is quite a bit of preparation that goes into those briefings . . . I know that you have not

agreed with many of the changes I've implemented in IICD and that you have close relationships with some members of IICD who have had performance and conduct issues that I've had to address. I hate having to address these issues, but it was necessary and I appreciate your support as I try to move IICD forward. IICD is moving in the right direction and I have received positive feedback internally and externally and what reflects positively on IICD, also reflects positively on you. When we succeed together, the success is ours to share. I'd really like to see, and I am very much open to feedback, how we can get to a better place because I value you and your leadership and experience, and I'd like to learn from you.[18]

Schneider responded that my "perception was just that" and that we were "actually on the same page."[19] I nonetheless did meet with her the next day. I went into the meeting with a plan and specific asks.

I walked into her brightly lit office, which was diagonally across from mine, a notebook in hand. This time I would be the one with the written talking points. Upon entering, I was hit in the face with the sweet smell of her incense infuser, a scent I was beginning to associate with mean girl bullying and everything wrong with the Capitol Police. Schneider sat at her desk, taking a moment before looking up at me from her computer.

During the meeting she said that she didn't understand why I thought she didn't support me. I responded by reminding her that back in January, she had told me that I should go back to doing things the way they had done before I arrived and that I held the staff to too high of a standard. I interpreted all that to mean that she didn't like how I was managing the team.

She said my perception of the conversation we had in January was "wrong."

That conversation with her back in January was what had prompted me to seek whistleblower protection.

Without prompting, I took the seat in front of her desk, shifting it to the right so that I could meet her eyes unobstructed by her computer screen. I reiterated what I had put in my email. "When you are copied on an email and the analyst is clearly being inappropriate, I really need for you to speak up and support me," I told her.

She refused. "I'm not here to tell employees they aren't behaving appropriately. But I could be a resource for you if you are having difficulty dealing with an employee." She added, "I don't understand why you go to HR and [the Office of General Counsel] when you have issues with employees. You can come to me first."

I didn't say anything to that because her response demonstrated that she didn't understand why I had reservations about going to her with personnel issues on the team.

I trudged on.

"I'd really appreciate it if you could provide space at meetings for all the divisions to brief." This was not an outlandish request, but by asking I was implying that she wasn't doing her job, at least not doing it well. At the time she was still the acting deputy chief of the Protective Services Bureau. She'd hold meetings with the leadership of IICD, the Investigations Division and the Dignitary Protection Division (DPD), but would only discuss or be interested in things related to DPD because that was what she knew, as her regular job was as the head that division. She would not ask if anyone had anything else to share.

Not surprisingly, she was defensive in her response. "I already do provide space in meetings for people to share."

I expected that's how she would respond, so I provided her with an example from a few days earlier. I politely pointed out that at our last meeting, she did not go around and ask for brief outs from two of the three divisions within PSB. "I had items to share with the other divisions and was not given a chance to speak."

She said that I should have spoken up if I had something to say. She was trying to turn it around on me. To her, this was my shortcoming, not hers. I didn't press on with the topic. The message had been sent.

For my final request, I set it up by saying that she was now the acting deputy chief and therefore needed to attend the biweekly briefings if for no other reason than to show the other members of the leadership team that she was supportive and understood the importance of the intelligence division, which now fell under her purview. She responded by saying that she would try to attend when she could. It was better than nothing.

But as the weeks went by, she only attended one briefing. Soon thereafter, she left the Capitol Police for a job with the Senate Sergeant-at-Arms after being passed over for the Deputy Chief and Chief of Police positions. In her new role, she tried to dictate to me how I should interact with the Sergeant-at-Arms office and with members of Congress. She sent one of her subordinates to my office with a list of things I needed to do to better serve her in her new role. The staff member was apologetic, and I recognized the politics at play. Before agreeing to any of the changes, I told Sean Gallagher. He reminded me that Schneider no longer worked for the Capitol Police and wasn't in a position to dictate to me how I should do my job. After that, I never heard more of her suggestions, nor did I ever meet with her again. Two weeks before her probationary period at the Sergeant-at-Arms office was up, she abruptly left.

Going forward, the changes necessary to establish a viable intelligence apparatus within the Capitol Police would need to come from my perseverance alone as support would be limited, but transformation would be expected.

ELEVEN

Regrouped and Reinvigorated

The aftermath of the insurrection left many Americans wondering how the greatest country in the world could become a place where some of its citizens would advocate for the power of a would-be dictator.

As was the case after the Oklahoma City bombing, the government became heavily refocused on domestic terrorism after January 6. The 2017 Unite the Right rally in Charlottesville had first brought the threat of extremism to the attention of the US government and the American people, but what happened at the Capitol would place it firmly in the spotlight. In March 2021, Department of Homeland Security Secretary Alejandro Mayorkas declared that domestic extremism "poses the most lethal and persistent terrorism-related threat to the homeland today."[1]

While Trump and his inner circle tried to hold on to the

presidency right up until Biden's inauguration—and Trump continues to peddle his "big lie" that the election was stolen from him to the present day—many of the extremist groups and conspiracy theorists who supported the insurrection have been forced to change their methods since January 6, 2021. For some groups, the insurrection has proven to be a boon, while others have seen their membership and influence wane.

While the number of extremist groups has actually decreased since January 6, 2021, from 159 in 2020 to fifty-six in 2022, according to the Armed Conflict Location & Event Data Project (ACLED), those that remain are just as dangerous, maybe even more so.[2] For example, demonstrations involving far-right groups—militia, white supremacists, etc.— are five times more likely to turn violent.[3] And despite the reduction in their overall number, demonstrations involving white supremacist groups actually increased by six percent in 2022. Overall, 21 percent of all demonstrations that include far-right groups also involve white supremacists.[4] The groups that remain active today have become more vocal and prone to violence, as well as more embedded with white supremacist and antisemitic elements. The prevalence of white supremacy and antisemitism make for a dangerous combination. In 2021, nearly 65 percent of hate crimes targeted victims due to their race, ethnicity, or ancestry and most were committed by a white person.[5]

One group that has kept growing since January 6 is the Proud Boys, with the group expanding from forty-three chapters nationwide in 2020 to seventy-eight in 2023.[6] January 6 was a recruitment bonanza for the group. Some of this growth can be attributed to the group aligning itself with other far-right elements and "normalizing their place within mainstream right-wing spaces" including inserting themselves into political causes important to the right. Some examples are attending school board meetings where the issue of critical race theory is being discussed and providing security at prayer vigils in front of abortion clinics, among others.[7]

But the numbers don't tell the whole story. Following the arrest of many of its leaders, the Proud Boys have experienced near constant infighting and power struggles since January 6. In the days after the insurrection, several local chapters said they were cutting ties with the national group, including chapters in Seattle, Las Vegas, Indiana, and Alabama. Many of the local chapters also denounced the Proud Boys' national leader, Erique Tarrio,[8] though his status was already on shaky ground after it had been revealed in court documents that he had been an informant for several law enforcement agencies.[9]

This leadership vacuum resulted in violent jockeying for power within the group. In the early hours of November 4,

2021, following Trump's speech in which he claimed that the election had been stolen, several Proud Boys, including Tarrio, were stabbed following an altercation outside the White House. Following this, Kyle Chapman, who had previously been a member of the Proud Boys but had been kicked out after being arrested at a Trump rally in Berkeley, California, in 2017,[10] tried to take over the group, citing what he believed to be Tarrio's cowardice during the November 4 violence. Chapman said he wanted to organize the group around fighting against "white genocide."[11] He was ultimately unsuccessful in his leadership quest. In January 2022, Chapman was arrested for assaulting a healthcare worker.[12] He was eventually sentenced to ninety days in jail and ordered to pay restitution to the victim.[13]

The direction in which Chapman wanted to lead the group was indicative of a development that became apparent after the insurrection, though it had been slowly building even before then: an increasing openness to white supremacy. As the Oath Keepers leader Stewart Rhodes noted, he had broken with the Proud Boys because the group was becoming more associated with white supremacy. This direction was confirmed by Tarrio himself. In January 2022, while he was in prison, Tarrio's Telegram channel began to feature a series of postings showing a countdown. Was this a countdown to a large Proud Boys demonstration, a big announcement, some violent act? Not knowing what it meant, I asked two of the agents who worked for me at the Capitol Police to interview Tarrio. In speaking with him, they discovered that the countdown was a reference to the date when he believed he would be released from prison (though unbeknownst to him at the time, he was to be released earlier than he expected). But during the interview, Tarrio also shared that the Proud Boys were heading in a more racially motivated direction.[14]

In September 2022, the Proud Boys held their annual meeting in Las Vegas. There, schisms in the organization became apparent, with roughly half of the members identifying as "standard" Proud Boys and the rest as "national." The "standard" group wanted to maintain the Proud Boys values, but with a more decentralized structure. The "national" group wanted to keep a hierarchical structure intact, with national leadership dictating the overall direction of the group. The two sides disparaged one another both at the meeting and online. This split between "standard" and "national" mirrored actions taken in Florida after Tarrio was revealed as an informant. The South Florida chapter, which Tarrio had overseen, split into two groups—"Villain City" and "Vice City."[15]

Unlike the Proud Boys, the Oath Keepers have seen their fortunes dramatically fall since January 6. With the group's leader, Stewart Rhodes, now serving a lengthy prison sentence for seditious conspiracy, the organization has lost its way. Though militia groups remain active in the United States, and there are some localized chapters of the Oath Keepers that continue to operate, the group is largely scattered and disorganized. A loosely knit conglomeration to begin with, the Oath Keepers now have no leader and no direction.[16] How they, and other militia groups, will evolve in the future remains to be seen.

Many white supremacist groups also saw changes after January 6, but it was more in how they portrayed themselves rather than in any alterations of their organizing structures. As noted in chapter three, groups like Patriot Front and NSC-131 have engaged in activities intended to improve their popular reputations, such as removing graffiti from murals, holding food drives, handing out care packages to the homeless, and cleaning up litter. By involving themselves in so-called legitimate acts of service, they are trying to endear themselves to their local communities, in the process making themselves appear neither dangerous nor problematic.

In this vein, the official White Lives Matter channel on Gab said in January 2023 that, "Shouts, honks, waves, thumbs up, every other person gave us a positive response. They loved us. The tides are turning. Our people are racially aware, they just need some encouragement . . . There's nothing to stop you."[17] But, dig further though their social media, and you will still see the usual hate, such as this post from January 19, 2023: "The extreme evil of the jew/communist/

faggot agenda . . . The US government, and the courts, are our enemies. That won't change until a new system is put in place."[18]

The rise in white supremacy is apparent in the massive surge of propaganda distributed by these groups, with 2022 seeing an all-time high of propaganda incidents, up by nearly 2,000 incidents from the year before.[19] And although there were more than fifty white supremacist groups that distributed propaganda material, 93 percent of the recorded propaganda incidents were perpetrated by just three groups: Patriot Front, White Lives Matter, and the Goyim Defense League. [20]

QAnon, although still in existence, has lost much of its allure since January 6, not because its ideology has been discredited, but because it has gone mainstream. After the insurrection and Trump's failure to be reinstated as president, QAnon adherents devised several other wild conspiracies, though Q himself largely remained silent. (There were over 5,000 posts from Q between October 2017 and December 2020, then little else until November 2022.[21]) One of the group's outlandish claims was that Biden's body was to be switched with Trump's at the inauguration ceremony and thus the "true" president would prevail. When that didn't happen, the Q conspiracists theorized that Trump would be made president again on March 4, 2021, the original date of the inauguration before it was moved in 1933 to January.[22] Time and time again, the goalposts were moved when the conspiracy didn't come to pass.

When Q finally posted some new "breadcrumbs" in November 2022, just before the midterm elections, the reaction from the QAnon community was decisively humdrum. Q had lost his luster, not because his followers had lost interest in conspiracy theories, but because the movement's ideology had integrated itself into the mainstream. A 2022 study found that 19 percent of Americans believed in at least some of the group's theories. The survey respondents were asked about their beliefs in three areas: that the government and other elites were Satanic pedophiles who trafficked in children; that a "storm" would come to remove the elites from power; and that it was up to American patriots to save the country.[23] Nearly three quarters of those who held these views identified as Republican or independent; only nineteen percent were Democrats.

Conspiracies surrounding election fraud and a government controlled by elites lend themselves to further, politically-fueled conspiracies. From Hunter Biden's laptop to Trump's multiple indictments, Republicans have decried efforts to apply the rules of democracy and law as "an intolerable state of weaponized politicization."[24] Robert Draper in his book, *Weapons of Mass Delusion: When the Republican Party Lost Its Mind*, postulates that it is a sense of righteousness—and transversely the presence of evil—that allows so many Republicans to embrace concepts that deviate from facts and reality.[25] In a survey conducted by the Public Religion Research Institute, 29 percent of participants identified as Christian nationalists or as sympathizers of Christian nationalist, most of whom identify as Republicans. Overwhelmingly, these two groups supported concepts such as "If the United States moves away from Christian foundations, we won't have a country anymore" and "Being a Christian is an important part of being truly American."[26] Recognizing this belief system helps us to understand how the Republican Party has come to embrace outlandish conspiracies. It is their fight against the evil forces trying to shape America.

Like with their leader Q, QAnon adherents have also largely moved on from Trump in order to focus on new causes such as Covid conspiracies and protesting drag shows.[27] QAnon has always been politically motivated, but today it is more focused on issues than people. The Anti-Defamation League warns that QAnon is becoming increasingly antisemitic, though there has always been an underlying thread of antisemitism due to the group's belief that the government is controlled by Jews.[28]

While groups like the Patriot Front attempt public outreach through volunteer work in their communities, others on the far-right have taken a more insidious route to mainstream acceptance. Anita Chabria of the *Los Angeles Times* spoke of "groomer" theories dominating the dialogue surrounding white supremacy and antisemitism—theories centering around protecting family values by supporting traditional gender roles (i.e., the alpha male, the subservient female), anti-abortion rights, and supposed threats from the LGBTQ+ community.[29] One need only take a glance at the social media of the far-right to see this. Below is an example from a neo-Nazi on the social media platform Gab that emphasized what they consider to be ideal gender roles:[30]

These core concepts are prevalent amongst white supremacist and neo-Nazi groups.[31] By focusing on the promotion of their definition of traditional family values and gaining the support of the general public in the process, it is less of a leap to push people toward more hateful beliefs. And it is having an effect. In 2022, there were twenty incidents from far-right groups targeting the LGBTQ+ community, up from seven in 2021.[32] By all accounts that number has increased in 2023. Drastically. In a report released by the Department of Homeland Security on May 11, 2023, they warned of increased threats of violence against the LGBTQ.[33] Furthermore, in 2023, there were more than 300 anti-LGBTQ bills introduced throughout the country.[34] NSC-131 targeted a LGBTQ+ event in Jamaica Plain—the section of Boston where I used to live—in July 2022,[35] and did the same on June 22, 2023, in Concord, New Hampshire.[36]

Today, hate speech is being permitted under the guise of freedom of speech. When public figures such as Elon Musk justify the inclusion of hate leaders like Trump, Andrew Tate, and Andrew Anglin on social media platforms and condemn calls for policing these platforms as "political correctness," they are endorsing and facilitating hate.[37] This is a dangerous road that can lead to violence, whether committed by an individual such as with Peyton Gendron in Buffalo, or as a group, as was the case on January 6, 2021.

But even if people like Musk were to apply more rigorous moderation policies to the platforms they control, these extremist ideas are still impossible to snuff out. Parler, the social media platform that was prolific before January 6, is a perfect example. After the insurrection, Amazon Web Services removed the site from its server. The platform eventually found a new home at Epik, which also hosts other fringe social media platforms like Gab. But by then, those who had been active on Parler had already migrated to other platforms, notably Telegram and Gab. Fighting hate online in many ways remains a game of whack-a-mole.

Beyond their search for a more acceptable form of online hate speech, some on the far-right have decided to work on seizing the political system through more traditional means. Since the insurrection, there has been a huge influx of candidates for office who hold extreme right-wing views. During the 2022 election cycle, the Southern Poverty Law Center tracked ninety-nine candidates with ties to extremism. This included twenty-three candidates who endorsed white supremacy or anti-immigrant rhetoric. Ten of these candidates won their races. They included: Wendy Rogers (Arizona State Senate), Paul Gosar (US House of Representatives), Marjorie Taylor Greene (US House of Representatives), Check Jenkins (Frederick County, Maryland Sheriff), Kris Kobach (Kansas Attorney General), Sam Page (Rockingham County, North Carolina Sheriff), Scott Perry (US House of Representatives), Brian Babin (US House of Representatives), Beth Van Duyne (US House of Representatives), and Dan Patrick (Texas Lieutenant Governor).[38]

Public office isn't the only part of the state apparatus

where extremism exists. As discussed in chapter three, it is also prevalent within the military. In its July 2022 report, the Profiles of Individual Radicalization in the United States (PRIUS) documented 545 cases from 1990 to July 2022 of extremism involving current or former members of the military. Just under half of these cases involved a premediated act of violence. Fifteen percent of those arrested were active-duty members at the time they were charged. About a third of those charged were affiliated with a white supremacist group.[39]

In December 2021, the Department of Defense issued a report outlining the steps it had taken to address the issue of extremism in its ranks. While the military did have some infrastructure in place surrounding the issue of extremism prior to January 6, one of the more important things it did following the insurrection was to update its definition of prohibited extremist activity. Department of Defense Instruction 1325.06 is broad and includes:

"Advocating or engaging in unlawful force, unlawful violence, or other illegal means to deprive individuals of their rights under the United States Constitution or the laws of the United States;" "advocating or engaging in unlawful force or violence to achieve goals that are political, religious, discriminatory, or ideological in nature;" "advocating, engaging in, or supporting terrorism, within the United States or abroad;"

"advocating, engaging in, or supporting the overthrow of the government of the United States . . . by force or violence; or seeking to alter the form of these governments by unconstitutional or other unlawful means (e.g., sedition);" "advocating or encouraging military, civilian, or contractor personnel within the DoD or United States Coast Guard to violate the laws of the United States . . . or to disobey lawful orders or regulations, for the purpose of disrupting military activities (e,g., subversion), or personally undertaking the same;" and "advocating widespread unlawful discrimination based on race, color, national origin, religion, sex (including pregnancy), gender identity, or sexual orientation."[40]

The instructions also include specific information on what constitutes "active participation." Overall, it is broad enough to cover most of the activities we saw on January 6 as well as behavior outside of participation in an insurrection. It is now up to the Department of Defense to enforce this rule. Statistics on how often this rule has been applied since it went into effect are difficult to find, but in an analysis of court filings, media reports and studies, the *Boston Globe* counted 260 cases involving active and former service members and extremism since 2018, with 178 of those cases involving those who were arrested for their participation in the January 6 insurrection.[41]

Enforcement should be a matter of urgency. Extremist groups can clean up as much graffiti as they like or run as many traditional election campaigns as they can organize, but they are still by their nature violent actors.

TWELVE

Investigations and Testimony

In the months following the insurrection, the Capitol Police's Inspector General began issuing "flash reports" focusing on different divisions within the organization, including the intelligence division. The final report would be issued in December 2021.

This wasn't the first time the Inspector General had audited the IICD. In March 2016, the IG had issued a report which concluded that the division lacked adequate internal controls. Specifically, the report said that IICD did not maintain up-to-date guidance or use standard operating procedures.[1]

The 2016 review also found that IICD didn't comply with policies related to the dissemination of information or procedures related to the SCIF, the use of classified systems and the handling of classified information, among other things. When I took over as acting director nearly five years later, these problems were still evident. For example, there were non-secure cameras that could be purchased at any office supply store connected to the computers in the SCIF, which was a security violation. I had the cameras removed, but I was astonished that they had been there in the first place.

The division I inherited also lacked guidance on collecting intelligence from open sources, as I have mentioned, and had not established mechanisms for evaluating workforce initiatives or the quality of the work products to ensure that they met the needs of the Capitol Police. Bluntly, the team was a mess, and it was obvious that none of the IG's recommendations from 2016 had been implemented.

Of the nine "flash" reports that the IG issued following the insurrection, two focused specifically on intelligence. Flash Report A looked at the intersection of operational planning and intelligence. Considering that this was the first report issued, it demonstrated that the Inspector General clearly recognized the failure to operationalize the intelligence the Capitol Police had received prior to January 6. The IG found that "[t]he Department lacked adequate guidance for operational planning."[2] The Capitol Police have three bureaus responsible for its operations: the Command and Coordination Bureau, the Uniformed Services Bureau (USB), and the Operational Services Bureau. All three fall under the Assistant Chief for Uniformed Operations, who on January 6 was Chad Thomas.

In preparation for protecting congress from an insurrection, the USB had only a one-and-a-half page "USB Operational Posture" plan, and it, like my intelligence assessment, had never been communicated to the officers on the ground ahead of January 6.[3]

I sat down with the staff at the Office of the Inspector General, offering testimony about IICD's role leading up to the insurrection. In the end, the office made sixteen recommendations related to intelligence. (I had suggested a number of these recommendations myself to the IG). They included:

- Revising guidance related to on-call personnel in IICD.
- Revising the intelligence priorities framework.
- Periodically reviewing the intelligence priorities framework.
- Increasing IICD staff.
- Obtaining security clearances for officers.
- Developing a cyber-intelligence task force.
- Establishing an intelligence bureau, rather than division, at the Capitol Police.
- Creating a training program for intelligence analysts.
- Writing guidelines on disseminating intelligence.
- Issuing guidance requiring Task Force Officers to

communicate intelligence to their commanders.

- Finalizing the Standard Operating Procedures about monitoring and reporting on First Amendment-protected demonstrations.
- Ensuring consistent and unified operational reporting across all intelligence and event planning documents.
- Including threat analysis in operational planning.
- Refining document reporting that captures the operational impact of the intelligence.
- Implementing guidance to provide consistency in intelligence products.
- Developing a forty-five—day action plan that included a gap analysis, training standards, a revised organizational chart, security clearance requirements and needed technology tools to improve intelligence capabilities.

I felt that many of these recommendations could be the impetus for the changes in the IICD that were very much needed. My hope was that by having an independent party make these recommendations, I wouldn't be looked at as the bad guy when I went about implementing them.

Even before the IG's flash report, several of the actions needed to fulfill the recommendations were already in the works. For example, one of the first things I did when I got to the Capitol Police (USCP) was to review all the guidance documents that were applicable to my team. Many of the documents were outdated and had not been revised in several years. The guidance about on-call personnel, for instance, was no longer relevant because IICD was now working on a 24/7 schedule. In addition, in reference to the recommendation on procedures for monitoring and reporting on demonstrations, I had drafted new procedures before January 6 because I was concerned that the team was monitoring US citizens who were engaged in peaceful First Amendment-protected activities. Relatedly, the team was also keeping photos of citizens in a folder on the share drive. I immediately put a stop to this, deleted the folder and its contents and instructed the team to no longer collect or keep this type of information.

The IG also recommended that the "Capitol Police provide training to its personnel on how better to understand and interpret intelligence assessments." Intelligence has its own language, and while I did think the assessment I wrote on January 3, 2021, was comprehensive and catered to its audience, namely the USCP workforce, the overall analysis had been at the end of the assessment. While this was not an unusual place for it to be in an intelligence product, the Capitol Police, at least those few who received the report, weren't accustomed to having to read finished intelligence products. Part of that goes to the prior points that the team didn't produce quality products, didn't traditionally adhere to analytic standards and often missed the mark in terms of relevance and accuracy in their assessments.

The IG's second flash report recommended that IICD complete periodic evaluations of its Intelligence Priorities Framework. The Framework contains a list of topics and areas that are considered a priority for intelligence collection. The USCP's Framework, which long predated my arrival, had never been reviewed, and a quarterly report, as required, had never been issued. I revised the guidance, putting the priorities in line with those issued by the Office of the Director of National Intelligence. I also completed the first ever quarterly review report.

The IG also recommended an increase in staffing for the intelligence division. This recommendation was essential, and having the IG make it, rather than me complaining that we didn't have enough staffing to adequately support and fulfill IICD's mission, placed the USCP leadership in a position where it needed to either increase its staffing or state in writing why it would not comply with the recommendation.

Ultimately, during my time at the Capitol Police, I implemented nearly all of the IG's recommendations for the IICD. I developed a training program for all analysts, which covered basic intelligence analysis, critical thinking, analytic writing, counterterrorism, open-source intelligence and instruction on internal systems. I called these "foundational" trainings because I didn't want to offend the analysts who had been with IICD for years and had never taken such courses. The more seasoned analysts were also required to take an advanced counterterrorism course, cyber security training and advanced intelligence analysis techniques. Within a year of my starting at the IICD, all the analysts had completed the required trainings, something that had not happened in the two decades prior to my arrival.

During January and February of 2021, there were a series of congressional hearings, with members of Congress—and the American people—demanding answers about January 6. Steven Sund had been forced to resign as Chief of Police the day after the insurrection, leaving Yogananda Pittman to serve as acting chief, and to have to answer many of the questions left in Sund's wake.

The House Appropriations Committee held the first public hearing on the insurrection in late January 2021. Conceding that the Capitol Police had not prepared adequately, Pittman apologized for the Department's failure and said that she and others within the leadership ranks knew "there was a strong potential for violence and that Congress was the target."[4] This was likely the most candid testimony provided by the Capitol Police about January 6.

In late February, the Senate Committee on Homeland Security and Governmental Affairs held its own hearing. Sund, former House Sergeant-at-Arms Paul Irving and former Senate Sergeant-at-Arms Michael Stenger, among others, testified. Sund and Irving primarily pinned the failures of January 6 on the supposed lack of intelligence, with Sund stating that the "[t]he breach of the United States Capitol was not the result of poor planning or failure to contain a demonstration gone wrong . . . Without the intelligence to properly prepare, the USCP was significantly outnumbered and left to defend the Capitol against an extremely violent mob."[5]

Irving provided similar testimony, reiterating the false belief that the January 6 rally would be no different than the first two MAGA rallies. Though, like Sund, he shared that he also thought there had been an intelligence failure, much of his testimony focused on defending the accusation that he had denied the request for the National Guard due to the optics, claiming that House Speaker Nancy Pelosi didn't like the look of having the National Guard at the Capitol.[6]

However, based on a conversation I had with then Speaker Pelosi about the September 18, 2021, "Look Ahead America"* demonstration, it was clear that she hadn't been fully briefed ahead of January 6. At the conclusion of the briefing with her about the September demonstration—and all the intel and possible scenarios of how that day could play out—she said to

---

*. Look Ahead America was a far-right organization that primarily advocated for the release of those charged in the insurrection.

me, "Why didn't I get a briefing like that before January 6?" I
told her that I didn't know.

Two days after Sund's testimony, Pittman testified before
the House Subcommittee on the Legislative Branch. She
struck a more positive tone this time, largely whitewashing the
reality of what had happened on January 6, stating in written
testimony, "But at the end of the day, the USCP succeeded in
its mission."[7]

Pittman highlighted the intelligence assessment I had
written as evidence that the USCP was prepared for January
6. However, intelligence serves an advisory function. It is not
operational. Having the information and acting upon it are
two different things. Pittman emphasized the intelligence to
shadow the failure of operationalizing it. That wasn't necessarily
her fault. In her role on January 6, she did not have command
over the officers and did not direct operational planning.

Pittman also discussed additional actions she claimed
the USCP had taken to prepare for January 6 based on the
intelligence it had. She wrote, for example, that the USCP
increased the size of the security detail for congressional
leadership from four agents to six. This was true, but only
for some members of the leadership, as several already had
six agents assigned to their details. Pittman also wrote that
she had directed agents to guard "the residence of certain
congressional leaders," but this wasn't something new or
done due to the upcoming January 6 events. Some leaders

residences were already being monitored, or had additional monitoring added, due to recent protests and vandalization of their homes.[8] She also said that the Investigations Division and IICD had extended their work schedule to twenty-four—hours a day. This was true for the Investigations Division, but IICD had been operating on a 24/7 schedule for several months before January 6.

Much of what Pittman discussed in her testimony were not additional steps related to intelligence about what might happen on January 6, but were routine actions that would be put in place for any large event. It reminded me of when I worked on implementing Trump's many Executive Orders as my agency's representative on the DHS transition team in 2017. Back then, I took several of the items that had been started under the Obama administration and repackaged them to appear to be fulfilling Trump's mandates. I saw a parallel effort in Pittman's testimony. She took things the Department was already doing to create the appearance the Capitol Police were more on top on things ahead of January 6 than it actually had been.

In March 2021, the Senate released its report on the insurrection. It acknowledged that the intelligence was supposed "to inform USCP's security and operational planning," but then went on to say that IICD failed to fully incorporate information about threats of violence focused on the January 6 Joint Session of Congress and the Capitol Complex. The report also said that large crowds had been expected to gather in DC on January 6.[9] While with the benefit of hindsight, I would have worded or emphasized things differently, all that information was present in the final intelligence assessment. Further, what wasn't in the formal assessment had been communicated in writing to USCP leadership.

The Senate report also overemphasized IICD's capabilities, with Steven Sund telling the investigators that the division was "comprised of approximately thirty to thirty-five analysts." In fact, IICD had eleven analysts on and before January 6.[10] It is telling that the head of the Capitol Police, who would later blame IICD for the failures that caused the insurrection, wasn't even sure how many people worked in the Department's intelligence unit.

Other elements of the Senate report were frustrating to me because they were correct, and I had sadly experienced them first-hand. For example, it was noted how the Capitol Police leadership "never took control of the radio system to communicate orders to front-line officers." I'll never forget listening to the radio throughout the whole ordeal, hearing officers screaming and dispatchers yelling, while the leadership remained silent.

The Senate report made sixty-five recommendations, nine of which were related to intelligence. The majority of these nine recommendations reflected efforts that were already underway before the insurrection, including revision and adherence to existing guidance, development of new guidance materials and additional training for analysts. Many of the changes I sought to make within IICD, and for which I was receiving severe pushback, pertained to these very areas.

It was a Sunday night in late March 2021. I was taking a rare moment to relax and watch television. Suddenly my phone, sitting on the coffee table strewn with clippings of construction paper left over from my daughters' art project, buzzed, alerting me to a text message. Steven Sund was texting me, asking if we could speak. As I sat on the sofa, I wondered why he wanted to talk to me, several months after he had stepped aside as USCP Chief. I texted him back saying okay and a few minutes later he called.

He asked me how I was doing, and we chatted for a bit about how things were going at the Capitol Police since he left. His voice was calm and friendly. After exchanging a few more pleasantries, he finally asked, "Was there something I missed?"

I immediately questioned the motivation behind his question. In his testimony before the Senate, he had said that

[a] clear lack of accurate and complete intelligence across several federal agencies contributed to this event and not poor planning by the Capitol Police. We rely

on accurate information from our federal security partners to help develop effective security plans. The intelligence that we based our planning on indicated that the January 6th protests were expected to be like the previous MAGA rallies in 2020 that drew tens of thousands of participants.[11]

After blaming intelligence officials like me for what had happened, was he now starting to question his own actions?

I didn't answer his question directly but instead told him the story of going up to the command center on January 6 and being so worried about what I was seeing that I made sure that my children left the city. How did he not see the same thing I saw, especially considering all the intelligence I had provided? Did he miss something? Yes, I thought to myself, he missed all the words I wrote warning of the potential for danger. Yes, he missed all the briefings where I gave warning of war.

"Why did no one tell me this?" he said, referring to what happened on January 6.

"I'm not sure why." I didn't know what else to say. I found it exceptionally difficult to believe that no one had told him anything to give him even an inkling of what was coming. The information was there. It was available to him. Some of it was sent directly to him. He had an obligation as the Chief of Police to heed what he heard. Why he didn't hear it or why he didn't take it seriously, I'll never know. That is for him to ask and answer for himself.

As the end of 2021 rolled around, I was still in the acting director position at IICD. The interview to get the job permanently was scheduled for the same week that I provided sworn testimony to the House Select Committee to Investigate the January 6th Attack on the United States Capitol and sat for an interview with CBS. I was also deathly ill that week and would eventually land in the hospital for several days. I had literally worked myself until I collapsed.

Despite my (noncontagious) sickly state, I was eager to tell my story. On a sunny December afternoon, I entered a television studio in southeast Washington, DC. The Capitol Police's Public Information Officer (PIO) was already there when I arrived. In the days preceding the interview, the PIO had prepped me on what to say. He explained that I didn't need to get into the nitty gritty of the problems I had experienced with my team. I was to stay on topic and just talk about January 6 and the intelligence assessment I had written.

The studio was open, with cameras and lighting equipment off to one side, and was staged to look like a living room, with a bookcase in the background. The interview lasted for nearly an hour. While there was much I wanted to say about the dysfunction of the intelligence unit and the lack of support I had inside and outside of the Capitol Police, I was still employed by the Department, and had to be careful about what I shared.

When the interview finally aired on January 5, 2022, only a few minutes out of the hour I had spoken was shown. Some of the things I said had been edited out of context, which was disappointing. For example, when I said I couldn't discuss personnel issues, I was referencing the problems with my team. When the story aired, though, it tied my statement about personnel to the larger criticism that Yogananda Pittman was still employed by the Capitol Police. Pittman had not been a thought in my head when I had given my answer. But this interview, like others I would give, was an example of how what you say and what you mean can be misconstrued very easily by those giving the final report.

In the months following the interview, my words would frequently be used against me. The employees I terminated used the statements I had made in the interview in their lawsuit. The GOP "shadow committee" would try to establish that because I said during the interview that "I knew things were not going to be good that day,"[12] that meant that I understood beforehand how bad it was going to be and did nothing to warn anyone.

To my friends and family, however, I was a minor celebrity and my actions ahead of January 6 were not in question. People from Stoneham, Massachusetts—unless you were ice skater Nancy Kerrigan—weren't usually on national television. At my grandmother's funeral, more than one person excitedly recounted how they had seen me on television. My aunt said the interview was good, but that I should have worn more eye makeup. A friend didn't like the way I wore my hair. Complaining about my hair and makeup was refreshing because to the people close to me, those were the main issues, not the content of the interview. They never questioned my integrity. They always knew I did what was right even when there were times that I felt the world doubted me.

That same week in December 2021, I met with the House Select Committee. Again, I was appreciative of the opportunity to tell my story.

I have never spoken to any of the congressional members on the committee. I also did not know any of the staffers who interviewed me. This was part of the reason I found it perplexing that Steven Sund would later say that "the J6 Committee's position continues to shield those in charge of intelligence [at the Capitol Police]."[13] If I were being shielded, it was without my knowledge and it certainly did not feel like anyone was protecting me from the negative attention I had received in the wake of the insurrection.

I also voluntarily spoke to the GOP's January 6 "shadow committee" on March 15, 2022. I knew the committee had previously interviewed the IICD employees I had terminated, so I wanted the members of the committee to understand that my actions were well-reasoned and appropriate. I was sure they thought that I was some left-wing radical, and I wanted to show them that I wasn't the person being depicted in the media.

During my interview, they asked some questions about the information I had ahead of January 6, but their focus was on the personnel issues within the team and its organizational structure. They wanted to know, for example, if the performance and disciplinary issues I'd had to deal with were a distraction from my duties. I told them that that came with the territory of any supervisory position. Though that was true, it was rare that a team would be so resistant to improving its performance that fifty-five percent of its personnel would have to be fired, transferred or otherwise pushed out.

The committee also focused on a *Politico* article, published in January 2021, which contained multiple accusations against me. The sources for the article, which were unnamed, were in fact three of the employees I had terminated. Despite me telling *Politico* that its sources were disgruntled employees, it went ahead and published the piece, which contained false and misleading information. The co-author of the article told the Capitol Police's PIO that he was "going to get those employees their job back."[14] The PIO lodged a complaint with the reporter's editor, but the article was still published.

One of the many accusations in the article against me was that IICD was writing dossiers on political donors at my direction, in particular for Senator Rick Scott of Florida. In truth, Senator Scott himself had requested intelligence assessments on private meetings he had had with several donors.

He also provided the names of the donors and their addresses. When IICD completed the intelligence assessment for Scott, it also conducted a Google search of any non-staff member who had attended the donor meeting, providing a one- or two-sentence biographic description of each person. A few words about someone's publicly available biographic description were hardly a dossier.

In May 2021, the IG released a report on the allegations in the *Politico* article. With regards to the dossiers, the *Politico* authors had written: "Among those who have been subject to new Capitol Police scrutiny are Hill staffers . . ."[15] In response to that allegation, the IG found that, "IICD will perform a Google search for any event participants listed on the request form but would not intentionally search congressional staff, which would only happen if any staff members were listed as participants and not known by IICD or identified as staff."[16]

In a similar vein, the *Politico* article had stated that "Farnam directed analysts to run 'background checks' on people whom lawmakers planned to meet, including donors and associates."[17] This was a reference to a commercial database used by law enforcement and others which contains addresses, phone numbers, driver's license information, criminal histories and social media, among other things. IICD will use this database if someone who has made a threat lives near an event location—it does not use it for completing an assessment on meetings attended by congressional members.

And this is exactly what the IG's investigation found: "Our work revealed evidence of IICD researching [a background check database] when completing assessments for threat/DOI notifications. Our work did not reveal evidence of IICD using [a background check database] when completing any other type of assessment."[18]

One accusation in the *Politico* article especially upset me because it should not have taken any sort of internal investigation to know it wasn't true. The article claimed that, "[a]nalysts also were tasked with sifting through tax and real estate records to find out who owned the properties that lawmakers visited."[19] In response, the IG found that "IICD doesn't check tax records because those records are not public and it does not have access to them ... Our work did not reveal evidence of IICD researching tax and non-public real estate records ..."[20]

In total, there were eleven allegations made against me in the *Politico* article, all based on accusations made by the same employees who I had terminated. In each case, the IG cleared me.

These allegations, though they had nothing to do with January 6, were nevertheless repeated in the "shadow committee's" final report, which stated that the *Politico* article raised "specific constitutional and civil liberties concerns."[21] The report was notable for omitting facts that did not fit its narrative. Though it cited the *Politico* article extensively, notably absent was any mention of the Inspector General's report that reviewed the allegations contained in the article.

When the committee released its report on December 21, 2022, it focused primarily on me, and my perceived failures, with my name appearing more frequently than Trump's, as if I was more culpable for the January 6 attack than the former president himself. The report was reflective of the ax the committee members had to grind with me and did little to forward the narrative of what had really happened on January 6, 2021.

I found out the report had been released not because anyone at the Capitol Police or on the committee shared a courtesy copy with me, but when a reporter—who had received an advance copy—called asking for comment. I asked her to send the report to me, which she did. I quickly scanned the document and became livid. The rage wasn't so much because the report was mainly about me, but instead concerned the commitment to lies, and the lack of integrity from our elected officials and their staffers. Their poor performance was the real failure the report showcased.

The terminated employees who spoke to the media—and later the "shadow committee"—to complain about me were not, as a group, media or politically savvy. As a result, I believed that they were being coached by someone with connections on the Hill—someone who didn't like me.

Kimberley Schneider had been USCP's Public Information

Officer prior to becoming head of the Dignitary Protection Division. Schneider was also close friends with Jeffrey "JJ" Pickett, a former Deputy Chief at the Capitol Police, who wrote two "whistleblower" letters to congressional leadership after January 6.[22, 23] The first letter was made up of several pages of ramblings about who deserved praise within the Capitol Police and who did not. Part of the letter discussed the perceived intelligence failures on January 6. (Throughout the letter, Pickett referred to the division by the wrong name, calling it IIAD.) He wrote that,

> It was reported to one of the subordinate commanders of IIAD [*author note: this is a reference to me*] by the Special Events Section, that the demonstration permits for those groups surrounding the Capitol on the 6th were all facades for Stop the Steal. This letter was corroborated by the intelligence analysis. The fact that IIAD was provided information that Stop the Steal was surrounding the Capitol from every side by separate entities was never relayed to operational commanders.[24]

As discussed earlier in the book, I had notified USCP leadership in writing of my concern about the groups and Stop the Steal on December 31, 2021.

Pickett also complained that IICD's intelligence assessment

didn't contain "critical information." However, he got several pieces of critical information wrong himself, such as the name of the division. He also wrote that the overall analysis paragraph that included my stark warning about the violence was on page fifteen; it was in fact on page thirteen. He also wrote that my assessment highlighted "issues the USCP would face was perhaps counter demonstrators clashing with the group." It did not. He also claimed that the assessment listed a remote possibility of violence, but he was actually referencing a completely different document.[25]

Pickett wrote a second letter in November 2021, after his first letter failed to garner the reaction he had presumably hoped for. This letter was sent to the congressional oversight committees and was primarily about the failures of myself and Sean Gallagher. The letter discussed specific personnel issues within IICD, information Pickett wouldn't necessarily have known on his own. One of the examples he provided as proof of my "harassment" of employees was an incident involving an analyst on my team who I'd had the local police department conduct a wellness check on after they failed to show up for work and could not be contacted.[26]

Despite his criticism of me and my actions, Pickett himself was not at the Capitol at the height of the fighting on January 6, 2021. Instead, he was the Deputy Chief in charge of the Capitol Police's training division, based out of Cheltenham, Maryland. After January 6, he was tasked with coordinating the administrative needs of the National Guard. He retired soon thereafter, after being passed over for the Chief of Police position.

Like the "shadow committee's" report, Pickett's letters had little to do with what had occurred on January 6. However, both were used, albeit unsuccessfully, to try and establish that I was incompetent and that my incompetence was what had led to the Capitol Police being blindsided by an angry mob of insurrectionists.

After Kimberly Schneider left the Capitol Police, I moved into her old office. It was twice the size of my old office and was bright with plenty of natural light. Because of our contentious relationship, it felt good to take ownership over something that had once belonged to Schneider.

I was sitting at my desk on February 15, 2022, reviewing an assessment the team had written, when a lieutenant from the Investigations Division came into my office.

"Shane Lamond," he said.

The name caught my attention. As far as everyone in the office was concerned, I barely knew Shane, and definitely not outside of work. We had actually stopped seeing each other romantically, though we continued to talk regularly for work, and he was still someone I considered a friend. "What about Shane Lamond?" I asked.

"He was arrested."

"Oh. That's not good. What for?" I later found out he had not been arrested, but, after his phone had been seized by the FBI, he had been suspended from his job pending the outcome of an investigation. I knew about the phone being subpoenaed and the grand jury, but that had all been several months ago. I had assumed that Shane was upset about the request to turn over his phone on principle, like it was an invasion of his privacy. I should have suspected there was more to the story.

"You probably need to find someone else in MPD to get your intel from now," the lieutenant added.

I knew that I immediately needed to let the FBI know of the conversations I had had with Shane about Tarrio, and about our relationship. They probably already knew about the relationship, but I'd rather they heard it directly from me than reading the text messages where Shane called me "Sunshine."

I was planning to call the FBI and disclose the relationship the next day, but Shane texted me first that evening.

"Hey Julie, can you talk?"

"Give me ten minutes," I replied. I didn't know what he wanted to talk about, but I needed some time to figure out what to do.

During those ten minutes, I called the FBI. The supervisor I spoke with sounded a bit amused when I told him everything about me and Shane.

"Should I call him or not?" I asked the supervisor when I was done. I wanted clear guidance on how to handle the situation. I was sure the supervisor had dealt with people whose ex-lovers were caught up with the FBI all the time. This was something new to me. I wanted him to tell me what to do and I would do it. Instead, he said, "I can't tell you what to do."

I decided to call Shane to hear what he had to say, with the intention of keeping the conversation brief.

"So, you remember that grand jury subpoena?" he began. "Well, I thought it had gone away because I hadn't heard anything in months, but I guess it didn't go away. The FBI came to my house yesterday and took my personal phone and work phone. They took away my police powers after that."

"I'm sorry to hear that," I said, not sure of how to respond to that limited admission. I also didn't want to get into the details with him. I already knew more than I wanted to.

"I didn't do anything wrong."

Right or wrong, I didn't want to be involved. This was yet another stressor on my already untenable interlude at the Capitol Police.

"I won't be able to respond to your work emails anymore and I don't have my phone. I didn't want you to think I was ignoring you." His words were soft spoken. He was not his usual, confident self.

The whole conversation lasted less than two minutes.

A couple of weeks later, on February 28, 2022, I got a call from an FBI agent asking to interview me. Later that same day I found myself in a tiny room with two female agents. The room had two windows, and though it was a sunny day, the blinds were drawn. There was a desk, but it didn't have a computer on it and on the side of the room were several chairs haphazardly placed that looked like they were being stored, rather than used. I detailed to the agents what Shane had told me about Tarrio. That evening, I sent the agents screen shots of all the communications I had had with Shane about Tarrio and the Proud Boys. I offered them all my text messages with him, but they just wanted the ones pertinent to their investigation.

I didn't hear anything more until September 1, 2022, when the FBI asked me if, in the days immediately following the insurrection, I had provided a list of names to Shane of individuals who had been identified as having been inside the Capitol building on January 6. They had a text message from Shane asking me for the names. I had in fact provided them to Shane, but not before asking the FBI back in January 2021 if it was okay to do so. It wasn't an unusual request. In the initial stages of the investigation into the insurrection, many agencies, particularly the Capitol Police and MPD, were collectively working to identify suspects. Sharing names was important because it helped to ensure we weren't duplicating efforts to try to identify someone who had already been identified. Shane was the only person I really knew at the Metropolitan Police—and at that point we were not romantically involved—so if I shared information with MPD, it would have been through Shane. But when the FBI asked me that question, it occurred to me that maybe Shane had only pursued me because of the information I had access to.

After he was placed on leave and later during the Proud Boys' seditious conspiracy trial, I learned just how closely Shane had been working with Enrique Tarrio. He reportedly gave the Proud Boys' leader advance notice that he was going to be arrested.[27] Shane had also shared the same information with me and expressed that I should keep it "close hold." (*Close hold* is government speak. It refers to something that shouldn't be shared unless there is an absolute need-to-know). It was also discovered that he was communicating with other extremist groups.[28] It seemed as if Shane was doing far more than gathering information; he was colluding with the enemy, if true.

I felt betrayed. The irony was that I had gone on that first date with Shane because I wanted to get information from him and build a bridge of communication. I never realized that he had had the same idea, but for far different and darker reasons.

Yogananda Pittman called me into her office one day in February 2022. I expected that she was going to give me a decision about the IICD director's position that I had interviewed for in December. Her office was on the seventh floor of the Capitol

Police headquarters and was decorated with photos of herself in uniform and trinkets from her college sorority. Videos from cameras throughout the Capitol Complex played on a television screen that hung on the wall to the right of her desk. I sat down at a small round table in the corner.

"For you it's about the work, but the politics around here . . ." Pittman told me while explaining why I didn't get the director's job. She talked about how I was valued, and that she hoped that despite not getting the job, I'd stay on and help the new director.

"Was it a man you hired?" I asked.

"I can't tell you that." (Ravi Satkalmi, a man, would be hired as director.)

I was done with all this. "I am being fucked after all I've done for this place!" I exclaimed. Then I stood up and left her office.

I was hurt and angry. But once I got over those feelings, a huge sense of relief washed over me. A weight had been lifted. I stopped worrying about the job and instead started to think about all the things I had postponed in the past year which I could do now that I didn't have to deal with the unrelenting bombardment of chaos and misery that I'd had to endure every day since January 6, 2021. It was now all someone else's problem.

I also felt a deep sense of pride, knowing that I had achieved a lot in my time with the Capitol Police. I had expanded the size of the team threefold, revised all the guidance documents, written new standard operating procedures, revised the position descriptions for the analysts to match those used in the executive branch, provided performance standards for the employees for the first time ever, and had removed all the poor performing employees. The personnel changes alone had made the experience worth it because it allowed me to hire talented, knowledgeable staff. It also sent the message that mediocrity no longer reigned supreme at the IICD.

My work as acting director of IICD had often come down to a choice between doing what was right and doing what was politically advantageous. Most of the time, those two things were not one and the same. It was not that I lacked political savvy or that I didn't understand the larger forces at play within the division and at the Capitol Police. I did, but I often made an affirmative choice to do what I thought was right and in the best interest of my team and its mission. That sometimes made me unpopular on Capitol Hill—and within my own team. It was a consequence I was willing to accept. It is also a choice that the Capitol Police would be wise to employ more often than they do.

After Ravi Satkalmi was hired, I went back to my old position as assistant director. By the spring of 2022, over a year removed from the insurrection, I was starting to see some of the Capitol Police's old ways start to creep back in. While there had definitely been changes within the Department, most had been concrete things—new plans, revised operating procedures, new equipment and training for the officers. Tangible items that could be touched, handled, and quantified. The real changes that needed to be made were non-tangibles, namely the culture of the organization.

In March 2022, the Capitol Police began to monitor the movements of the truckers—or People's—convoy as it looped around Washington, DC, and Maryland, in case it ended up at the Capitol. To provide updates to those who had a need-to-know, someone in the Command and Coordination Bureau set up an email distribution list. When I asked that the supervisors with the Dignitary Protection Division (DPD) be added to the list—because that team drove congressional leadership all over the city and thus might be impacted by the convoy—I was met with resistance. "We should discuss how the [distribution list] works with intel and command center information in/outflows. We are finding everyone wants to be on this list . . ."[29] one commander complained.

This was a commander who had been working on January 6, and he was now advocating for not sharing information. The Capitol Police had already played the game of not communicating and not sharing information . . . and had lost, badly.

I quickly drafted a fiery response but put the message aside before sending it. I usually had the presence of mind to cool down before sending angry emails, though anger was very much justified in this situation. I ultimately did not send the message but did raise my concerns to the Capitol Police leadership. More importantly, I ignored the suggestion to limit the number of people receiving information and forwarded the emails to the DPD. I would not withhold information from those who needed it the most.

This was not the only example of the Capitol Police reverting to its old ways. In July 2022, the Government Accountability Office sent the Department an information request for an audit it was doing regarding the events of January 6. The request included the question, "Please describe why USCP did not determine threats (e.g., threat identified by USCP or shared with USCP) were credible for the events of January 6." They were asking this question because Yogananda Pittman had stated under oath in February 2021 that "the Department was not ignorant of intelligence indicating an attack of the size and scale we encountered on the sixth. There was no such intelligence. Although we knew the likelihood for violence by extremists, no credible threat indicated that tens of thousands would attack the US Capitol."[30]

The original response the USCP drafted in response to the GAO request stated that it did not view the intelligence as credible. When I pushed back, asserting that there was most definitely credible intelligence and pointing out the reason why the GAO was likely asking this question—because Pittman had said there had *no* credible intelligence—the Capitol Police had Ravi Satkalmi, who had not been employed by the Department on January 6, 2021, rewrite the response. He wrote that, "We respectfully disagree with the premise of this question. We did enhance our preparations as we learned more about the threat landscape on Jan. 6. For example, we increased our staffing, modified our security perimeter, and undertook other operational security measures in response."[31] Having someone who had not been working for the Capitol Police on January 6, and who had no firsthand knowledge of the events of the day, write about how the Department perceived the intelligence it had received ahead of the insurrection, was insulting. And it was wrong. The longer I stayed at the Capitol Police, the more infuriated I became with how the Department was trying to whitewash what had happened.

I spoke with my attorney, who arranged a secret meeting between me and the GAO. I was tired of not being heard, of not having a voice in the story of January 6, of telling the truth and having it dismissed. I provided the GAO with over fifty pieces of raw intelligence that had been given to the Capitol Police leadership ahead of January 6, along with a timeline of when it was received.

The GAO issued its report about the attack on the Capitol in February 2022, and it was one of the few reports that came out in the wake of January 6 to acknowledge that the intelligence was accurate, and had been sent to the Capitol Police leadership.

The report also captured the flawed approach the Department had taken in communicating about and preparing for that day:

> The Capitol Police's planning for January 6 was similar to how it planned for the previous MAGA marches held in November and December 2020, which Capitol Police documents indicated had the potential to become violent but ultimately were largely non-violent within the Capitol complex . . . While the initial special event assessment started with drawing similarities to the MAGA marches of November and December 2020, the subsequent assessments evolved as more intelligence was gathered, and ultimately noted how January 6 may be different from those previous marches, particularly in regard to the potential for violence.[32]

Reading this, I cracked a slight grin. It was a small acknowledgment of my efforts, and for that I felt grateful. It also represented a glimmer of hope that perhaps there were people out there who wanted to uncover the truth of what had led to the insurrection, a truth that was often buried under a mountain of falsehoods and misrepresentations.

THIRTEEN

Countering Extremism

A commitment to extremist ideology, or a belief in conspiracy theories, doesn't happen overnight. Someone just doesn't wake up one day and decide they are a neo-Nazi, for example. It takes time to get from what we would consider normal beliefs to a radical ideology. Similarly, the jump from believing in a cause to committing violence in the name of that cause is also a gradual process.

The first step on the path to radicalization is a grievance: discontent with a religious, political, or social situation. With domestic extremism, most of the grievances surround the social/racial (e.g., white people are being replaced) or political (e.g., elections are not fair). These grievances open the door to wanting to find solutions to the perceived problem. As the National Institute of Justice explains, at the "pre-radicalization" stage, an individual may start expressing disillusionment with their grievance, which leads them to seek out more information about it.[1] Part of this information seeking is trying to find others who are fighting to address the same grievance.[2] This in turn leads the individual to join a like-minded gang, terrorist organization, or extremist group. Whether the driving force is disillusionment, a personal crisis,[3] or moral disgust,[4] some type of emotional void generally propels people to find interest and comfort in extreme and violent ideologies. Those who radicalize have a hole in their lives they are attempting to fill.

As discussed previously, many extremist groups try to tap into this emotional void by marketing themselves to susceptible individuals with polished videos, pictures, and choreographed marches that celebrate their cause. For example, white supremacist groups like Patriot Front engage in high profile rallies and other activities with the intent of not only spreading their ideology, but also recruiting new members. They march through cities in formation, setting off red, white, and blue smoke flares while they film themselves. The videos are then edited for maximum inspiration and uploaded to social media platforms such as Telegram, Gab, and Odysee. It is propaganda, and it is attractive to vulnerable individuals looking for purpose and community. The images are also deliberately crafted to appeal to the target audience—mainly young white men.[5] (Recruitment videos for the Rise Above Movement show muscled young men working out in sunny California.) Al-Qaeda has long successfully engaged in this practice, with slick publications written in the language of their intended audience, and videos intended to inspire people to want to join their cause. Whether it is a foreign group like al-Qaeda or a domestic group like Patriot Front, the propaganda is designed to pique interest.

The next stage in the radicalization process is detachment. This may include actions like spending more time with similarly-minded individuals or groups, making lifestyle changes, or trying to convince others to follow the ideology.[6] But before one can become detached, the ideology must become hardened within the person, often by a technique known as "gradually scaling commitments."[7] As al-Qaeda and other terrorist groups have found, coming on too strong at first can deter individuals from joining the group or advancing the ideology. By gaining commitments incrementally, the individual is slowly brought into the fold; with each progressive commitment, they move one step closer to radicalization and violence.

A key step toward making extremism more acceptable to a vulnerable person who isn't necessarily looking to become a terrorist but is upset with the way they feel their race / religion is being treated, is normalization. Andrew Anglin, founder of the white supremacist / neo-Nazi website, The Daily Stormer, has openly pronounced that his goal is to "normalize our ideas, to get to the point where you can say these things that we believe in the open, publicly, without being physically attacked, without losing your job, without getting kicked off of the internet."[8]

Next comes "peer immersion."[9] This can include joining a community of other extremists. In the United States we have seen extremist groups like the Asatru Folk Assembly who go so far as to purchase property for their group members to gather at.[10] As discussed previously with Ruby Ridge, the area where Randy Weaver lived included a large concentration of followers of the Aryan Nations. Pockets of extremist communities exist throughout this country. In the peer immersion stage, someone wanting to be closer to an extremist group may choose to move to the community where the group is centered. This stage can also include participating in training with extremist peers. Many of the extremist groups previously mentioned such as the Rise Above Movement, the Three Percenters, NSC-131, all have trainings for their members.

The next step on the road to violence is planning. The "Pathway to Violence" model developed by Frederick Calhoun and Steve Weston in the early-2000s, demonstrates how what starts with a grievance progresses over time to violent ideation. This model has been adopted by the Department of Homeland Security to educate the public about how radicalization can lead to violence. As an example, Peyton Gendron, the Buffalo supermarket shooter, engaged in extensive planning not only in how he chose his target location, but also in the equipment he used. He even wrote a manifesto laying out his planning process.[11]

In November 2022, Terrorgram, a collective of white supremacist accelerationists, parodied the DHS's "Pathway to Violence" informational flier, which is intended to raise awareness about the steps one takes on their path to radicalization. The six steps listed in the flier are: grievance, violent ideation, reach and planning, preparation, probing and breaching, and then finally attack.[12] The Terrorgram network labeled their flyer, "Path to Sainthood." The final step was "sainthood achieved."[13]

There are several programs—both domestic and international— that provide opportunities to intervene before someone reaches the point of violent radicalization. In the United States, the *US Violent Extremist Mobilization Indicators* booklet, produced by the FBI, the Department of Homeland Security, and the National Counterterrorism Center in 2019, and revised in 2021, lists potential indicators to help friends, family, coworkers, and others recognize the signs that someone may be planning to make the leap from thinking or talking about violence to engaging in a violent act. The mobilization indicators include traveling to carry out or participate in violent extremist activity or conducting a dry run and surveilling targets; disposing of personal assets and saying goodbye or making post-death arrangements; and communicating the intent to commit violence and / or purchasing equipment and weapons. The individual may also develop a relationship with other extremists, isolate themselves, or seek technical expertise, among other actions. In all, the handbook list forty-two indicators to be on the lookout for.[14]

The Department of Homeland Security also hosts the Center for Prevention Programs and Partnerships (CP3), which seeks "to prevent acts of targeted violence and terrorism by working with the whole of society to establish and expand local prevention frameworks."[15] The program outlines five "core lines of effort," including coordinating and sharing resources by setting up personnel in the field, strategic engagement with a variety of stakeholders, helping to guide local prevention policies, offering grants to aid in prevention efforts, and promoting education and information sharing.[16]

In a similar vein is the Prevent program in the United Kingdom. The goal of the program is to stop "vulnerable people [from] being drawn into criminal behaviour."[17] Where the UK program differs from CP3 is that it focuses on getting the police involved before an individual becomes violent, since they may be the first to encounter someone going down a radicalized path. The police make referrals to Prevent. Part of the program focuses specifically on terrorism through its Counter Terrorism Advisory Network (CTAN). CTAN is like CP3 in that it provides community outreach, guidance in the development of prevention policies and other resources.

Other similar models exist elsewhere in the world. In Germany and Sweden, EXIT is designed to help stop the progression to violence by giving extremists a way out. The aim is to have the radicalized individual get to a place where they can engage in "critical reflection," in order to "challenge . . . the old ideology."[18] To achieve this, EXIT provides education to families, schools, first responders, and the larger community. EXIT also works with radicalized individuals to help alleviate their anxieties about departing from an ideology or extremist group by showing them how to change and experience fulfillment in their lives without the need for extremism.

Helping someone leave an extremist group or violent ideology requires understanding why they joined in the first place, as well as what keeps them committed. To be clear, most people who harbor extremist beliefs do not join extremist groups, nor do they commit violent acts. Belief alone is not enough to propel someone into terrorism. Multiple studies have shown that, much like why someone goes down the rabbit hole of conspiracy theories, "group membership can satisfy basic needs such as the need to feel valued and to be respected by others."[19] Joining an extremist group provides camaraderie and purpose. This is why programs such as EXIT or Prevent can be effective—they target the underlying reasons for joining an extremist group in the first place. They also help those with strong ideological convictions find value and purpose in their lives that does not require commitment to a violent group or ideology.

According to the FBI, the definition of international terrorism is "violent, criminal acts committed by individuals and/or groups who are inspired by, or associated with, designated foreign terrorist organizations or nations (state-sponsored)." Domestic terrorism, on the other hand, are "violent, criminal acts committed by individuals and/or groups to further ideological goals stemming from domestic influences, such as those of a political, religious, social, racial, or environmental nature."[20] Despite the different influences, the outcomes are the same: violence in support of an extremist ideology.

However, the strategies used in countering foreign terrorist organizations cannot be applied uniformly in the domestic terrorism context. Foreign terrorist organizations typically have a structure, leaders, and some type of financing. Domestic terrorists such as Peyton Gendron often work alone, or with limited interaction with others, and frequently lack resources. They are influenced by umbrella groups, be it anti-government, militia, or those that are racially/ethnically motivated, but are not necessarily inspired by a single leader. They do not take direction, other than gaining inspiration from those who have previously committed violence for the cause.

In the cases where there is a leadership structure, and it is dismantled, that doesn't always mean the group will disappear. The Proud Boys, for example, have not suffered an organizational crisis with the loss of its leadership, as we saw with the Oath Keepers. Though there has been infighting within the Proud

Boys with Enrique Tarrio no longer at the helm, the group continues to exist and evolve post-January 6. Removing the leadership of extremist groups creates a void that may or may not be filled, but it also does not erase the ideology that the group members believe.

The bigger challenge is stopping proxy leaders—those who inspire and mentor but are not necessarily the actual leader of the group. For example, James Mason is very influential when it comes to the current neo-Nazi movement. Mason is the author of *Siege*, a collection of essays published in the 1990s that discusses the so-called conspiracy among the government, capitalists, and Jews against white people. Mason draws inspiration from Hitler and Nazi Germany, as well as Charles Manson, who was a friend of his. Mason continues to advise and motivate a new generation of neo-Nazis. He is very much a leader in the ideological space, and while disrupting his sway would be beneficial, making him lose relevance is more difficult than simply removing a leader from power.

Reducing or eliminating influence is made harder by the internet and social media. It is relatively simple, for example, to find *Siege, Mein Kempf, The Turner Diaries,* and other examples of extremist writings online. Here is an example of one channel on Telegram making some of the most prominent white supremacist and neo-Nazi titles available for download. It took me less than a minute to locate these links:

This is a particular issue in the United States, which is predominant in propagating extremist discourse online. According to the RAND Corporation, "there has been a shift toward a post-organizational landscape that is made up of decentralized networks of small cells and lone actors."[21] This makes it more challenging for law enforcement to identify threats, particularly if these discussions occur through encrypted communications, or in the case of a lone wolf, without any communication.

One organization that is committed to "preventing terrorists and violent extremists from exploiting digital platforms" throughout the world is the Global Internet Forum to Counter Terrorism. The Forum is a conglomerate of technology companies, which collect images, videos, and texts that have been uploaded and shared by terrorist networks. Using this material, they work to identify trends and the locations of terrorists and terrorist groups. As the terrorist threat is always evolving, staying on top of what is being posted and shared online is a major step in preventing, responding to, and learning about, the groups and ideologies that may present danger.

Recognizing the risk factors, understanding the mobilization indicators, preventing the attraction of extremism in the first place, and intervening when violence is imminent are all necessary steps to try and prevent individuals from becoming radicalized.

But there is still more that can be done.

To truly counter the threat of domestic terrorism will take a multifaceted approach. Rather than looking at incidents on a case-by-case basis and charging participants with state-level offenses, there is a growing call in the United States to prosecute these cases at the federal level as civil right violations and hate crimes. This will take legislative changes and a commitment from the appropriate federal agencies to provide staffing and resources. As the Digital Citizens Alliance rightly concludes,

> while what amounts to domestic terrorism is defined in federal law, there are currently no specific penalties for engaging in it. Because of this gap, the actors who engage in violent acts designed to intimidate or coerce a civilian population, influence the police of government

by intimidation or coercion, or affect the conduct of a government by mass destruction, assassination, or kidnapping are not charged as domestic terrorists.[22]

And then there are the financial considerations. Many extremists raise money through crowdfunding, as the Proud Boys did in order for their members to come to Washington, DC, on January 6. Seizing or freezing the assets of these groups would be helpful in deterring the spread of hate. In the wake of the Unite the Right rally in Charlottesville, jurors found seventeen white nationalist leaders and organizers liable, resulting in a $26 million judgment.[23] New Hampshire has recently started to target NSC-131 and to ask the courts to impose fines against members of the group for doing such things as hanging "Keep New England White" banners on highway overpasses. Although the fine, if imposed by the judge, would not exceed $10,000,[24] it is a rather significant amount of money for most individual group members. Christopher Hood, the leader of the group, isn't independently wealthy and doesn't have meaningful employment. The group is also not known for its fundraising capabilities. Fining individual members and group leaders who have been convicted of crimes related to extremist ideology, although many are judgment-proof and would ultimately be unable to pay, still sends a powerful message.

Overall, as we have seen in this chapter, there are multiple techniques that have been shown to work to stop individuals from reaching the violent radicalization stage. We need not reinvent the wheel to prevent another January 6. However, we do need the courage to apply these strategies. Given our divisive political environment, truly battling domestic terrorism may prove to be a challenge this country is not ready to take on.

FOURTEEN

What Comes Next

In March 2021, the head of the FBI, Christopher Wray, told lawmakers that "January 6 was not an isolated event. The problem of domestic terrorism has been metastasizing across the country for a long time now and it's not going away anytime soon."[1] True to Wray's prediction, the problem has continued to grow. In December 2022, the Armed Conflict Location & Event Data Project (ACLED) noted that, "[a]fter the attack on the Capitol in January 2021 and through the November 2022 midterm elections, far-right mobilization has only continued to evolve in the United States."[2] ACLED went on to add that "white supremacy and white nationalism together constitute the most salient driver of far-right protest activity . . ."

Looking forward, Steven Simon of the MIT Center for International Studies and Jonathan Stevenson of the International Institute for Strategic Studies wrote that "[a]s the 2024 election approaches, the threat of political violence and civil breakdown is only going to increase. And despite all that U.S. national security and law enforcement officials have learned since Jan. 6, the country is still not prepared for a far-right revolt." Simon and Stevenson also believe that "large-scale civil collapse," does not require large groups, but that "spiraling acts of violence by small numbers of people that may originate spontaneously but, fueled by retaliation, [could] develop their own momentum." The results of this could be calamitous:

> Gradually escalating attacks triggered by key events and facilitated by the growing accumulation of privatized high-powered weapons like AR-15s, largely on the right, could increase polarization to a point of irreversibility. A contagion of localized but widespread tit-for-tat violence could produce mass abdications on the part of local law enforcement and overwhelm the capacity of the federal authorities, turning expanding pockets of U.S. territory into essentially Darwinian enclaves. Such a scenario—recall "Bleeding Kansas" in the 1850s—is broadly in line with the run-up to the Civil War. [3]

These frightening scenarios make it clear that without changing the path we are currently on related to domestic terrorism, two things are certain: there will be more violence and our democracy will be further eroded.

A positive first step in acknowledging the threat to our country was the White House's "National Strategy for Countering Domestic Terrorism." Released in June 2021, the document is a starting point to address the extremism and conspiracies currently bewitching the American public. The report identifies four pillars essential to addressing the domestic terror threat, including: understanding and sharing domestic terrorism-related information; preventing domestic terrorism recruitment and mobilization to violence; disrupting and deterring domestic terrorism activity; and confronting long-term contributors to domestic terrorism.[4]

The goals of the National Strategy are comprehensive, but there is still much more work to be done. To help address the blight caused by extremism and conspiracy theories in the United States today, I recommend the following:

Recommendation One: Create clear guidelines to ensure consistent collection and reporting of extremist activity that does not infringe upon the civil and privacy rights of Americans.

Traditionally, and some have argued this contributed to January 6, intelligence agencies have been reluctant to collect intelligence on domestic entities. Concerns over civil liberties and privacy rights have frequently hindered investigations, but that doesn't have to mean that protecting the rights of the

American people is incongruent with gathering intelligence on the extremists in our midst.

In the many meetings I have participated in with the FBI, they have always said that they do not monitor First Amendment-protected activities, even when there are concerns of violence or other unlawful activity at demonstrations. The same is true for online hate speech, which the intelligence community will not collect or report on because they believe it is constitutionally protected material.

To fulfill my recommendation, clear guideposts need to be set. There is a fine line between speech and actions that cross from First Amendment protection into criminality. In terms of speech, the line is often drawn at whether the words are designed to incite. Do they pose a threat to life? But like all things, context matters, which makes defining and interpreting hate speech problematic. The intelligence community thus needs specific national priorities that permit and designate the collection of intelligence related to domestic extremism.

In *The Ethics of Intelligence*, author Ross W. Bellaby outlines several elements that constitute an ethical intelligence framework: there needs to be just cause to investigate, legitimate authority, intentionality, proportionality, and targets should be legitimate (not overly broad).[5] In an essay on the ethics of risk management, Kevin Macnish also touches upon proportionality, writing that "intelligence activity should be proportionate in terms of the harms that it risks when balanced against the benefits that it promises."[6] We know the current limited posture with regards to intelligence and domestic terrorism is not sufficient to address the threats we face. However, the harm of doing too little outweighs the risks of not collecting intelligence.

Recommendation Two: Create stiffer penalties for those who perpetrate violence at protests or demonstrations.

The number of domestic terrorism incidents at demonstrations has steadily risen. In an analysis of 1,040 domestic terrorist attacks and plots, in 2019, only two percent occurred at a demonstration, but in 2020, it was nearly half. In 2021, it was 53 percent.[7] We have seen more frequent violence emerging out of protests, from both the far-right and the far-left. This is what happened on January 6. This is what happened in Portland, Oregon, in 2020. These demonstrations crossed the line from First Amendment freedom of assembly to becoming a violent threat to others. To be clear, I am not referring to non-violent civil disobedience—sitting in the middle of the road or chaining yourself to a fence. These tactics are more annoying than dangerous. I am talking instead about activities like breaking into buildings, threatening others, physically fighting, lighting items or buildings on fire, throwing objects, etc. This kind of activity should be subject to additional penalties when committed in conjunction with individuals who are trying to peacefully assert their First Amendment rights.

Americans should be able to exercise their rights under the First Amendment without fear. Being able to demonstrate and voice one's support or opposition or to push for reforms, rights, and justice is a fundamental entitlement in this country. There is no place for violence in that.

Accordingly, violence perpetrated at demonstrations or targeting demonstrators should be subject to stricter penalties under the law. As things stand now, those who engage in unlawful conduct at protests—be it fighting, looting, or destruction of property—are charged as someone would be regardless of the context of where the crime took place. Unlawful activity at a protest should result in an enhanced charge, making it a more serious offense.

Recommendation Three: Work with other governments to fight hate and track extremism, including designating more groups as terrorist organizations.

Strategic Goal 1.3 of the "National Strategy for Countering Domestic Terrorism" notes that "some domestic violent extremists have sought ties and connections to individual violent extremists overseas."[8] We've seen this with leaders of white supremacist groups fleeing the country, such as Rinaldo Nazzaro, leader of the neo-Nazi group The Base, who is believed to be in Russia.[9] We've also had internationally based extremist groups set up chapters in the United States. This includes the Soldiers of Odin, an organization based in Finland, which has established chapters in Montana, Pennsylvania, and Colorado.[10]

Despite these examples, most of the extremists operating in the United States today originated in this country. It is we who are outsourcing hate. The Proud Boys is one such example of a group that was started in the United States, albeit by a Canadian, and has spread to other countries, especially Canada, the United Kingdom, and Australia.[11] Other examples include the Three Percenters, the Atomwaffen Division, and The Base, which are US-based extremist groups that have been designated by other countries as terrorist organizations. As much as we seek information from foreign governments about extremist groups, we should also proactively share with other governments what we know about the groups operating here in the United States.

It is also not unheard of for a domestic extremist group to support a foreign terrorist organization. In 2022, two members of the Boogaloo Bois pleaded guilty to providing material support to Hamas, a designated foreign terrorist organization.[12] More commonly, however, domestic extremist groups will borrow tactics from foreign terrorist organizations as they look to them to gain inspiration, especially when their tactics have been successful in the past.

Recommendation Four: Congress and the White House must stop politicizing government agencies working to keep Americans safe.

When the Department of Homeland Security was

established in 2002, it was done so with the intent, above all else, to "prevent terrorist attacks within the United States."[13] Since its inception though, the threats have changed, while intelligence, in many ways, is still stuck in an early 2000s mindset.

DHS's intelligence shop, the Office of Intelligence and Analysis, or I&A as it is commonly referred to, is supposed to integrate and disseminate intelligence to protect the country, but it has frequently been swayed by the political winds. Notably, in 2009, it authored a report about domestic extremism and the efforts of extremist groups to recruit and infiltrate the US military. The report, advanced for its time, caused political outrage. Veterans' organizations and members of Congress alike decried the report for supposedly advancing the political agenda of the Obama administration.[14] This political pressure resulted in DHS stopping nearly all collection or reporting on domestic extremism for several years.[15] Ahead of January 6, DHS shared almost no information about the impending riot.

I&A's reputation has also not been helped by its focus on the far-left to the near exclusion of the far-right. During the summer of 2020, journalists who were reporting on the ongoing violence in Portland, Oregon, revealed leaked internal DHS documents written about antifa.[16] In retaliation, DHS is alleged to have compiled dossiers on the journalists. Rather than going after the journalists who had published the leaked document, DHS should have taken ownership over the reports and focused its energies on finding out who had internally supplied the documents to the journalists without authorization.

Trust in DHS's intelligence capabilities was severely undercut during the Trump administration when then-acting undersecretary for I&A, Brian Murphy, sought whistleblower protection after several incidents where he was asked to change or downplay important intelligence. For example, he was asked to embellish the numbers of known or suspected terrorists (KSTs) entering the United States via the southern border to support Trump's efforts to build a border wall. DHS reported at a congressional hearing that nearly 4,000 KSTs had crossed the border when the actual number was only three.[17] Murphy was also ordered to alter intelligence reports regarding conditions in certain Central American countries. He refused. Murphy was also asked to "cease providing intelligence assessments on the threat of Russian interference in the United States, and instead start reporting on interference activities by China and Iran."[18] When Murphy wrote a threat assessment on the rise of white supremacy in the United States, he was asked to focus more on left-wing groups. Again, he refused and was subsequently demoted.[19]

As the Center for a New American Security rightly points out, "the time has come for policymakers to decide what they want I&A to be and reduce the gap between the reality and perception of its authorities."[20] Like the Capitol Police, government organizations that are influenced by political whims lack integrity, and that impacts their missions and our safety. Fault for this lies not only with the individual agencies, but more importantly with Congress. In our deeply divided country, congress cannot "weaponize" government agencies. While it should rightfully question their actions and probe their policies, ultimately, congress must support the mission of DHS and other intelligence agencies.

Recommendation Five: Regulate social media content and create mandatory reporting.

All social media platforms operating in the United States must have clear and transparent content moderation policies, and violations involving unlawful content must be reported to law enforcement. Mark MacCarthy of Georgetown University argues that content moderation is essential and recommends "reconceptualizing the regulatory problem as one of consumer protection rather than content regulation."[21]

In 2022, I participated in a panel (along with Brian Murphy and others) at the Trust and Safety Professionals Association to discuss cooperation between social media companies and law enforcement. These companies are constantly removing content and suspending users due to violations of their policies. Despite the fact that some of this banned content constitutes illegal material, it is rarely turned over to law enforcement, which makes it untraceable should there be a threat. There have been several instances when I have gone to research a threat made against a member of Congress only to find that it has been removed from the social media site. Since it wasn't shared with anyone from law enforcement before its removal, it has effectively been wiped. (I have never had a social media company proactively send me or my office a threat.) Removing the material is a good first step, but it is vital to share the material with those who need to know.

Peyton Gendron posted his manifesto on social media days before he committed his violent, racist attack in Buffalo, which he livestreamed. In my time at the Department of Homeland Security, we regularly found social media content depicting assaults, drug use, and gang activity. At the Capitol Police, I viewed countless videos of violence posted on social media. Even the subject of the Netflix documentary, *Don't Fuck With Cats*, posted multiple videos of animal cruelty online before moving on to killing a person. Had any of these incidents been reported to law enforcement beforehand—and law enforcement responded appropriately—further threats to the safety of others could have been prevented.

Social media companies will counter that they are not in the business of determining what is or is not illegal content. This leaves it to congress to set a threshold for what must be reported. At a minimum, inciting violence, making threats to life, child pornography, murder, gang activity, trafficking, sexual assault, and animal cruelty should be reported when discovered by social media companies. This is not creating new categories of unlawfulness; it is taking things that if known to law enforcement would be illegal. When the social media platforms share this information, the onus will be on law enforcement to decide if they want to pursue charges or not. Social media platforms have demonstrated they cannot police themselves; therefore, the government has an obligation to step in and regulate the industry for the protection of the country and its citizens.

Reform would require amending Title 47 United States Code Section 230. This section of law says that "[n]o provider or user of an interactive computer service shall be treated as the publisher or speaker of any information provided by another information content provider."[22] The law effectively shields social media companies from liability when speech posted on their platforms contributes to harm.

Supporters of Section 230 believe that judicial or legislative intervention to change or limit the scope of the law would create a "risk of over-censorship."[23] This sentiment was shared in then-President Trump's May 2020 Executive Order where he directed the Federal Communications Commission to engage in rule-making to ensure that "[Section 230] is not distorted to provide liability protection for online platforms that—far from acting in 'good faith' to remove objectionable content—instead engage in deceptive or pretextual actions (often contrary to their stated terms of service) to stifle viewpoints with which they disagree." The Executive Order was advocating for platforms to be held liable when they removed content in a manner that the administration deemed to be biased.[24]

Determining when a social media company should be held liable for harmful content is for congress, or the courts, to decide. Two recent Supreme Court cases, *Twitter v. Taamneh* and *Gonzalez v. Google*, considered the issue of what, if any, legal responsibility social media companies have for the content on their platforms. Unfortunately, both cases ruled in favor of Section 230 and kept the lack of liability for social media companies in place. But as we see a propagation of social media platforms, many discussed in this book, that knowingly host inciting, unlawful and violent content, it is more difficult to argue these platforms are ignorant of what is being posted and oblivious to the damages it causes. There must be accountability.

Recommendation Six: Bar non-compliant social media platforms from operating in the United States.

Relatedly, social media platforms that refuse to establish content policies and refuse to moderate their users need to cease operations in the United States. Platforms such as Telegram, 4chan, Gab, and others must be held accountable for the content they are propagating under the guise of "free speech." Just as the United States contemplates banning TikTok because of foreign spying concerns, it should ban other platforms that pose a threat to public safety.

Recommendation Seven: Hold accountable politicians who support hate and conspiracies.

When a new member of Congress allegedly flashes a white power hand gesture on the House floor, that is something that needs to be addressed immediately, particularly by the party to which that member belongs.[25] Similarly, when a member of Congress repeats anti-Semitic tropes, it must be addressed directly and swiftly.[26] Other recent examples of politicians supporting hate or conspiracies include:

- In October 2020, then-Representative Madison Cawthorn verbally attacked a journalist who supported his opponent by saying the journalist was supporting, "non-white males, like Cory Booker, who aims to ruin white males running for office."[27]

- In February 2022, Representatives Marjorie Taylor Greene and Paul Gosar appeared at an America First Political Action conference, organized by Nick Fuentes, founder of the white supremacist group, the Groypers. At the conference, Nick Fuentes praised Adolf Hitler, yet both Greene and Gosar did nothing to refute or challenge Fuentes.[28]

- Joe Kent, who beat Representative Jaime Herrera Beutler in the 2022 primary, but lost the race, posed for a photo with a Nazi sympathizer who called Hitler an individual who "many people misunderstand." The chief strategist for Kent's campaign was Matt Braynard, the founder of Look Ahead America, an organization dedicated to advocating for the rights of those arrested for participation in the insurrection.[29]

- Senator J.D. Vance said that Democrats "have decided that they can't win reelection in 2022 unless they bring in a large number of new voters to replace the voters that are already here," playing into the sentiment that whites are being replaced by immigrants. The chair of the House Republican Conference, Elise Stefanick, has expressed similar sentiments.[30]

- After being asked if Hillary Clinton and the former heads of the CIA and FBI would be arrested, and if there should be mass resignations of Democrats in Congress, Representative Lauren Boebert reiterated the conspiracy theories by saying that "I heard from someone who is in very close contact with President Trump and the ins and outs of the White House under that administration . . . and this is my opinion with that information that I have, I believe we will see resignations begin to take place."[31]

- Representative Bob Good sponsored a bill that
  would "prohibit the indoctrination of racially
  divisive curriculum within our nation's schools."[32]
  Good also participated in the organizing of the
  MAGA rallies.[33]

The list goes on.

Voters have a responsibility to hold these politicians accountable by not voting for them in the first place or recalling them when they do spread hate. Congressional members have a responsibility to censure, penalize, and impeach their fellow lawmakers when necessary. Too often, though, congress is inclined to look the other way because they don't want to tip the power they hold in favor of the other party.

Recommendation Eight: Enact legislation targeting domestic extremism.

Following the Oklahoma City bombing in 1995, the conservative Heritage Foundation, critical of the Clinton administration, advocated that the government needed to do more to "stop terrorist attacks before they can be carried out, through preventive policies such as the infiltration of terrorist groups and improved intelligence-gathering on their activities."[34] They recommended easing intelligence guidelines to allow the government to gather more information about domestic terrorism groups and suspects. This was in sharp contrast to conservatives' position today.

In 2022, a bipartisan group of representatives introduced the Domestic Terrorism Prevention Act. The bill had seven main goals:

- Establish "requirements to expand the availability of information on domestic terrorism, as well as the relationship between domestic terrorism and hate crimes."

- Authorize domestic terrorism components within DHS, DOJ, and the FBI "to monitor, analyze, investigate, and prosecute domestic terrorism."

- Report "on domestic terrorism, including white-supremacist-related incidents or attempted incidents."

- Review "the anti-terrorism training and resource programs of their agencies that are provided to federal, state, local, and tribal law enforcement agencies."

- Make "training on prosecuting domestic terrorism available to its prosecutors and to assistant US attorneys."

- Create "an interagency task force to analyze and combat white supremacist and neo-Nazi infiltration of the uniformed services and federal law enforcement agencies."

- Assign an FBI "special agent or hate crimes liaison to each field office to investigate hate crimes incidents with a nexus to domestic terrorism."[35]

The bill passed the House in a largely party line vote, with only one Republican voting for it and four Republicans not voting at all. It then failed in the Senate, with Republicans blocking it, saying they believed the targeted departments and agencies already had the legislative authority to move forward with the authorizations outlined in the bill.

While Republicans in Congress may claim that legislation already exists to address the concerns outlined in the Domestic Terrorism Prevention Act, this was a cowardly excuse for failing to pass this bill. Republicans had the opportunity to state publicly that they take domestic terrorism seriously, and that hate should be challenged and prosecuted. They made the decision not to do that to the detriment of our country and our safety. The changes needed to address this scourge in the United States must have legislative backing. Extremists have become an unstoppable force against an immovable object. When will congress push back?

Recommendation Nine: Start a national campaign to raise awareness about mobilization to violence.

Like the "See Something, Say Something" campaign in the wake of 9/11, the United States needs a national campaign to raise awareness about domestic terrorism. One FBI agent who worked on the Oklahoma City bombing case said that "Tim McVeigh is the epitome of the lone wolf. But even a lone wolf still must be part of something that gets them to that point."[36] The *Mobilization Indicators* booklet, discussed in the previous chapter, is an important document, but with forty-two indicators, it's not easily or quickly digestible by the public. The government would be wise to highlight the most common indicators of potential violence and share how the general public can report their concerns. Simply put, the government must do more to raise awareness about domestic terrorism.

Recommendation Ten: Educate children to make them resilient to extremist ideology.

Hate starts at home. It is reinforced at school. To create long term change, children need to learn and understand that hate is wrong. It is both as simple and as difficult as that. As UNESCO has said, "Disarming the process of radicalization must begin with human rights and the rule of law, with dialogue across all boundary lines, by empowering all young women and men, and by starting as early as possible, on the benches of schools."[37] When efforts to educate children on the discrimination non-whites, non-Christians and others have faced throughout the history of the United States, parents, teachers, and politicians are met with fierce opposition. The opposition is denying children the opportunity to empathize with the adversity and struggles others have faced. This is not a "woke takeover of education" as the Heritage Foundation has declared.[38] It is basic humanity.

By barring children from the right to know and understand different perspectives, we are preventing healing the wrongs of the past, and allowing them to occur again in the future. The fact that so many feel threatened by a curriculum that tells the story of injustice demonstrates just how deeply ingrained that injustice is in our society. Such curriculum does not divide; it creates an opportunity to bring Americans closer together. Just as many conservatives in the United States are Christian, they must heed the Ninth Commandment—thou shall not bear false witness against thy neighbor. Denying the right to knowledge of different perspectives of peoples with whom we must coexist is a lie by omission and is fundamentally in contrast to true Christianity.

In hearing after hearing, the tears flowed. "I have paid a high price, and I accept that I still have to pay more . . . I hope that you and our country never have to face another day like January 6th," said the person who shot bear spray directly onto fifteen police officers on January 6. He received a sixty-eight-month prison sentence.[39] "Sadly, I partook in some idiotic actions that have changed my life forever," said the man who sprayed a fire extinguisher at the police.[40] He received a thirty-three-month sentence. "I made one mistake in my life and I have immediately took [sic] responsibility for it," another cried.[41] He was arrested a week after the riot, only after posting videos on Facebook bragging about the destruction he had caused. Many expressed regrets in public, but true repentance was less common. Derrick Evans apologized in court when being sentenced to prison for his role in the insurrection, but later claimed he was the victim of a political persecution.[42]

Remorse and accountability are difficult to find in the story of January 6. Steven Sund, who was responsible more than anyone at the Capitol Police for the failings on that day, has since tried to portray himself as a victim and a hero. As I replay in my mind what I could have said or done differently, many of the players from January 6 have focused more on deflection than self-reflection.

Sund seemed astonished that I was still in my position at the Capitol Police at the time of his book's publication in 2022. What he neglected to recognize, because he likely didn't have any visibility into it, was that the team was flourishing under my leadership. The IICD had grown by over three hundred percent and all the analysts had received extensive intelligence training. Our intelligence assessments were now sent directly to officers in the field. The daily intelligence report had been revamped. I had also implemented a daily intelligence briefing for leadership, and IICD now processed threat cases efficiently and accurately. Most importantly, we had earned the respect of the Department and of our intelligence and law enforcement peers. I did all of this to try to make the Capitol Police, members of Congress, and this country safer, despite the challenges I faced in doing so.

But it'll take more than reforms to intelligence analysis and more than changes within the Capitol Police to prevent another insurrection. To stem the violence, we as a country must take a stand against those who want to destroy us, including those from within. None of the solutions are easy, but the only way we can move forward is to address hate and conspiracies head on. From education to legislation to vigilance, all of us play a role in protecting our democracy. We cannot, and must not, let January 6 be the beginning of the end of this remarkable country.

By the time I left the Capitol Police in May 2023, the decision to go was an easy one. I had written my resignation letter a hundred times over in my head. Every time I had to listen to J. Thomas Manger, who had taken over as chief from Yogananda Pittman, stumble in answering why I was still in my job, or when I saw my name in print with the same false allegations, I wondered if change would ever come.

I put all the plants I had in my office into a box, packed up my books, and cleaned out the drawers of my desk. I was finally stepping off the roller coaster that I hadn't wanted to get on in the first place. What I was left with were memories of one of the darkest days in the history of this great nation, memories that will stay with me for the rest of my life. But more than that, I have a deep appreciation for our democracy, and I hold steadfast to the hope we can and will do better at protecting it in the future.

Author's Note
and Acknowledgments

Living the story conveyed in this book was a miserable experience. To see those whom I had trusted and admired betray me was disappointing and personally hurtful. After the phone call I had with Steven Sund that I recount in the book, I sent him a text message. I ended the message with words of comfort, writing, "I know it's hard now, but things will eventually get better."

By nature, I tend to be a trusting person. I take people at face value and give them the benefit of the doubt. I stay longer than I should in bad situations because I would rather strive to make them better than turn away from a challenge. I believe there is more good than bad in the world and each one of us has the ability to positively impact the domain around us. Those beliefs were tested in my time on Capitol Hill. There, in the bedrock of democracy, I found deep dysfunction on both sides of the aisle. I had many long-time staffers tell me it hadn't always been that way. When did so many members of Congress lose their integrity and character, and how do we get it back?

Maybe my former boss at the USCIS Boston District Office was right—I was put in that position at the Capitol Police for a reason. No one else was speaking up and telling the world what really happened on January 6, 2021. No one wanted to admit their faults and failures. Stories of heroism abound, as they should for those who fought gallantly, but a dark undercurrent of lies in the retelling of January 6 sought to wash away truth and justice.

As I raise my children, I hope to instill in them a sense of duty and personal responsibility, and to impart in them enough character to stand up in the face of brutal opposition and to have the strength to remain unflinching when others seek to silence what they know to be factual.

I owe much gratitude to the friends, family, and loved ones who not only supported me during the writing of this book, but who also comforted and encouraged me while I was living its story.

I am especially grateful to Timur for his love and support. He lived much of this story by my side and never wavered in his commitment to me. To Larissa, Michael, and Larry—thank you for reading and rereading chapter after chapter and providing your honest feedback. Thanks also goes to Jordan Mulligan for his expert editing.

This book would not have been realized without Robert Lasner and Elizabeth Clementson of Ig Publishing taking a chance on a woman with a story. And of course, Mark Zaid, my attorney and the man who keeps me out of trouble (or who bails me out when I do get in trouble).

And I cannot forget to thank the wonderful staff at the Tarbouch Café. Much of this book was written there, fueled by pots of mint tea, shish tawook, and shisha.

Notes

Introduction

1. Select Committee to Investigate the January 6th Attack on the United States Capitol, Transcribed Interview of Christopher Rodriguez, Jan. 25, 2022, 42:17–19.

2. Select Committee to Investigate the January 6th Attack on the United States Capitol, Transcribed Interview of Muriel Bowser (Jan. 12, 2022), at 50:17–19.

3. Select Committee, 50:15.

4. Select Committee, 50:15–16.

5. January 5, 2021, email from AOC Command Center re: Individual says "go to Washington Jan 6 and help storm the Capital" adds "we will storm the government buildings, kill cops, kill security guards, kill federal employees and agents": Blog via 8kun).

6. January 5, 2021, email from AOC Command Center.

7. January 5, 2021, email from AOC Command Center.

8. Select Committee to Investigate the January 6th Attack on the United States Capitol, Transcribed Interview of Steven Sund, (April 20, 2022), 39:14–15.

9. Select Committee to Investigate the January 6th Attack, 61:2–3.

10. Select Committee to Investigate the January 6th Attack, 75:24–25; 76:1–2.

11. Select Committee to Investigate the January 6th Attack, 79:6–14.

12. Select Committee to Investigate the January 6th Attack, 80:15–16.

13. Select Committee to Investigate the January 6th Attack on the United States Capitol, Transcribed Interview of Valerie Hasberry, (Apr. 14, 2022), 48:21–23.

14. Select Committee to Investigate the January 6th Attack, 53:3–4.

15. Select Committee to Investigate the January 6th Attack on the United States Capitol, Transcribed Interview of Steven Sund, (April 20, 2022), 67:14.

16. Select Committee to Investigate the January 6th Attack, 73:15–18.

17. Select Committee to Investigate the January 6th Attack, 73:19.

18. "Proud Boys Regroup, Focusing on School Boards and Town Councils," *New York Times*, December 14, 2021, https://www.nytimes.com/2021/12/14/us/proud-boys-local-issues.html.

One: Change and Resistance

1. Aaron C. Davis, "The Attack," *Washington Post*, October 31, 2021, https://www.washingtonpost.com/politics/interactive/2021/warnings-jan-6-insurrection/.

2. Norman C. Grahe, "IICD Transition," (email), November 3, 2020.

3. US House of Representatives GOP January 6th Shadow Committee, Report of Investigation: Security Failures at the United States Capitol on January 6, 2021, 117th Cong., 2022.

Two: The Gathering Storm

1. Rob Kuznia, Curt Devine, Nelli Black, and Drew Griffin, "Stop the Steal's Massive Disinformation Campaign Connected to Roger Stone," CNN, November 14, 2020, https://www.cnn.com/2020/11/13/business/stop-the-steal-disinformation-campaign-invs/index.html

2. Stop the Steal LLC, "Business Entity Records," State of Alabama, November 13, 2020, https://arc-sos.state.al.us/cgi/corpdetail.mbr/detail?corp=821150.

3. Sheera Frenkel, "The Rise and Fall of the 'Stop the Steal' Facebook Group," *New York Times*, November 5, 2020, https://www.nytimes.com/2020/11/05/technology/stop-the-steal-facebook-group.html.

4. Alabama Secretary of State, "Business Entity Search: Stop the

Steal," October 4, 2021, accessed June 24, 2023, https://arc-sos.state.al.us/cgi/corpdetail.mbr/detail?corp=000821150&page=name&file=D&type=ALL&status=ALL&place=ALL&city=.

5. Robert Glover, interview by Select Committee to Investigate the January 6th Attack on the Capitol, May 2, 2022.

6. Glover, May 2, 2022.

7. Intelligence and Interagency Coordination Division, "Million MAGA March," November 12, 2020, Washington, DC: United States Capitol Police.

8. Hannah Allam, "A March Without Millions Is Still A Worrying Sign Of A Nation Divided," *NPR*, November 15, 2020, https://www.npr.org/2020/11/15/935181031/a-march-without-millions-is-still-a-worrying-sign-of-a-nation-divided.

9. Carl von Clausewitz, *On War*, trans. Michael Eliot Howard (New Jersey: Princeton University Press, 1989).

10. Donald Trump, interview by *Fox & Friends*, Fox News, December 13, 2020.

11. Stephen Miller, interview by *Fox & Friends*, Fox News, December 14, 2020.

12. Kaylin Jorge, "Police: Explosion in Downtown Nashville Is Intentional, 41 Businesses Damaged," *WZTV Nashville*, December 25, 2020, https://fox17.com/news/local/explosion-reported-in-downtown-nashville-emergency-crews-on-scene-tennessee-christmas-morning-hotel-broadway-nissan.

13. AT&T, "Nashville Recovery Efforts," December 28, 2020, Accessed June 24, 2023, https://about.att.com/pages/disaster_relief/nashville.html.

14. Jacob Knutson, "Pelosi, McConnell Homes Vandalized," *Axios*, January 2, 2021. https://www.axios.com/2021/01/02/pelosi-mcconnell-homes-vandalized-stimulus.

15. Julie Farnam, "January 6th Protests-Areas 8-9," (email), December 31, 2020.

16. *United States of America v. Thomas Caldwell et al.*, 2022. 21-cr-28-APM Second Superseding Indictment United States District Court for the District of Columbia, January 8, 2022.

17. Intelligence and Interagency Coordination Division, "January

6, 2021 Joint Session of Congress Demonstrations," December 23, 2020. Washington, DC: United States Capitol Police.

Three: Forces at Play

1. *United States of America v. James Alex Fields Jr.*, 3:18CR00011 United States District Court for the Western District of Virginia Charlottesville Division, June 27, 2018.

2. Susan Milligan, "From Embrace to 'Replace'," *U.S. News and World Report*, May 20, 2022, https://www.usnews.com/news/the-report/articles/2022-05-20/the-republican-embrace-of-the-great-replacement-theory.

3. Simon Clark, "How White Supremacy Returned to Mainstream Politics," *Center for American Progress*, July 1, 2020, https://www.americanprogress.org/article/white-supremacy-returned-mainstream-politics.

4. Peyton Gendron, "You Wait for a Signal While Your People Wait for You." Manifesto, May 14 2022.

5. Anti-Defamation League, "Extremists Engage in Political Violence During Pro-Trump Rallies." January 6, 2021, accessed January 11, 2023, https://www.adl.org/resources/blog/extremists-engage-political-violence-during-pro-trump-rallies.

6. Vincent James, "The Red Elephants—Vincent James." *Bitchute*, March 2019. https://bitchute.com/channel/bWargwAUQYXi.

7. The Red Elephants, "The Red Elephants YouTube," *Gab*, December 2017, https://gab.com/TheRedElephants.

8. Vincent James, "Vincent James," *Telegram*, November 2019. https://t.me/RealVincentJames.

9. Southern Poverty Law Center, "VDARE," accessed January 11, 2023, https://splcenter.org/fighting-hate/extremist-files/group/vdare.

10. *Washington Post* Staff, "Identifying Far-Right Symbols that Appeared at the U.S. Capitol Riot," *Washington Post*, January 15, 2021, https://washingtonpost.com/nation/interactive/2021/far-right-symbols-capitol-riot/.

11. Center for Media and Democracy, "SourceWatch," June 8, 2022,

accessed January 11, 2023, https://sourcewatch.org/index.php/ DonorsTrust.

12. Donald J. Trump, "Presidential Bid Announcement Speech," New York, June 16, 2015.

13. Patriot Front (@PatriotFrontUpdates), "Activists from Network 11 Reprogrammed a Road Sign in Fargo, North Dakota," Telegram, January 3, 2023, https://web.telegram.org/z/#-1478154831.

14. Patriot Front (@PatriotFrontUpdates), "Activists from Network 7 Placed a Banner in Nashua, New Hampshire," Telegram, January 6, 2023, https://web.telegram.org/patriotfrontupdates.

15. Patriot Front (@PatriotFrontUpdates), "Activists Removed Obscene Graffiti from a Mural in Baltimore, Maryland," Telegram, January 8, 2023, https://web.telegram.org/z/#-1478154831.

16. Patriot Front (@PatriotFrontUpdates), "Activists Cleared Trails and Removed Litter from the Mount Baker Snoqualmie National Forest in Western Washington," Telegram, January 5, 2023, https:// web.telegram.org/z/#1478154831.

17. Patriot Front (@PatriotFrontUpdates), "Activists from Network 11 Held a Food Drive in Jamestown, North Dakota," Telegram, January 7, 2023, https://web.telegram.org/z/#-1478154831.

18. Patriot Front (@PatriotFrontUpdates), "Activists from Network 11 Handed Out Care Packages to the Homeless in Sioux Falls, South Dakota," Telegram, January 6. 2023, https://web.telegram. org/z/#-1478154831.

19. Anti-Defamation League., "National Socialist Club (NSC-131)," September 29, 2022, accessed January 19, 2023, https://adl.org/ resources/backgrounder/nationalist-social-club-nsc-131.

20. Associated Press, September 30, 2020, (YouTube video), 0:44 min. https://www.youtube.com/watch?v=qIHhB1ZMV_o.

21. David Gilmour, "Meet the Proud Boys, the Pro-Men, Anti-Masturbation Enemy of 'Antifa'," *The Daily Dot*, September 7, 2017, https://www.dailydot.com/layer8/proud-boys/.

22. Sammy Nickalls, "Why the Proud Boys Initiation Ritual Involves Cereal," MyRecipes.com, February 13, 2018, accessed

March 26, 2023, https://www.myrecipes.com/extracrispy/why-the-proud-boys-initiation-ritual-involves-cereal.

23. Alan Feuer, "Proud Boys Founder: How He Went From Brooklyn Hipster to Far-Right Provocateur," *New York Times*, October 16, 2018, https://nytimes.com/2018/10/16/nyregion/proud-boys-gavin-mcinnes.html.

24. Wilson, Jason. "Portland prepares for city's largest far-right rally of the Trump era." *The Guardian*, August 16, 2019. https://www.theguardian.com/us-news/2019/aug/15/portland-oregon-far-right-rally.

25. Donald J. Trump, "Memorandum on Inadmissibility of Persons Affiliated with Antifa Based on Organized Criminal Activity," official memorandum, Washington, DC: White House, 2021. https://trumpwhitehouse.archives.gov/presidential-actions/memorandum-inadmissibility-persons-affiliated-antifa-based-organized-criminal-activity/.

26. Immigration and Nationality Act, U.S.C. 8 § 1182(a)(3)(B)(iii) (1952).

27. Government of Canada, "Public Safety Canada," June 25, 2021, accessed December 6, 2022, https://www.publicsafety.gc.ca/cnt/ntnl-scrt/cntr-trrrsm/lstd-ntts/crrnt-lstd-ntts-en.aspx.

28. Nick Perry, "New Zealand Designates Proud Boys a Terrorist Organization., *AP News*, June 30, 2022, https://apnews.com/article/canada-religion-new-zealand-race-and-ethnicity-racial-injustice-aaf63aaa32fbe9ccd2d46e8ff5d417f3

Four: The Anti-Government

1. Peter Applebome, "Terror in Oklahoma: The Background; A Bombing Foretold, In Extreme-Right 'Bible'," *New York Times*, April 26, 1995, sec. A, page 22.

2. Anti-Defamation League, "*The Turner Diaries*," February 5, 2017, accessed January 25, 2023, www.adl.org/resources/backgrounder/turner-diaries.

3. Alexandra Alter, "How 'The Turner Diaries' Incites White Supremacists," *New York Times*, January 12, 2021, www.nytimes.com/2021/01/12/books/turner-diaries-white-supremacists.html.

4. Jason Wilson, "Ruby Ridge, 1992: the Day the American Militia Movement Was Born," *The Guardian*, August 26, 2017, www.theguardian.com/us-news/2017/aug/26/ruby-ridge-1992-modern-american-militia-charlottesville.

5. Catrina Doxsee, "Examining Extremism: The Militia Movement," August 12, 2021, accessed January 19, 2023, https://www.csis.org/blogs/examining-extremism/examining-extremism-militia-movement.

6. Elmer Stewart Rhodes III, interview by Select Committee to Investigate the January 6th Attack on the United States Capitol, February 2, 2022.

7. Spencer S. Hsu, Rachel Weiner, and Tom Jackman, "U.S.: Oath Keepers, Rhodes Attacked 'Bedrock of Democracy' on Jan. 6," *Washington Post*, October 3, 2022, https://www.washingtonpost.com/dc-md-va/2022/10/03/oath-keepers-trial-openings-rhodes/.

8. Ashley Swann, "Oath Keepers Guard Upstate Military Recruitment Centers," *WYFF*, July 22, 2015, https://www.wyff4.com/article/oath-keepers-guard-upstate-military-recruitment-centers/7016186.

9. Kyle Cheney, "Text Message Trove Shows Oath Keepers Discussing Security Details for Trump Associates," *Politico*, April 18, 2022, https://www.politico.com/news/2022/04/18/oath-keepers-security-trump-jan6-00026157.

10. *See* supra Note 6 (Rhodes III).

11. Joseph Nunn, "The Insurrection Act Explained," *Brennan Center for Justice*, April 21, 2022, https://www.brennancenter.org/our-work/research-reports/insurrection-act-explained.

12. *United States of America v. Elmer Stewart Rhodes III et al.,* 2022, 21-cr-15 (APM), Superseding Indictment United States District Court for the District of Columbia, January 12, 2022.

13. Anti-Defamation League, "The Oath Keepers Data Leak: Unmasking Extremism in Public Life," September 6, 2022, accessed January 19, 2023. https://www.adl.org/resources/report/oath-keepers-data-leak-unmasking-extremism-public-life.

14. Bob Christie, "Probe OK'd of Arizona Senator's Comments on Buffalo Shooting," *AP News*, May 25, 2022, https://apnews.com/article/donald-trump-wendy-rogers-phoenix-arizona-new-york-cf54a9bc2592edb5ede75eba02389ef3.

15. Robert Evans, "White Boy Summer, Nazi Memes and the Mainstreaming of White Supremacist Violence," July 1, 2021, accessed January 18, 2023, https://www.bellingcat.com/news/2021/07/01/white-boy-summer-nazi-memes-and-the-mainstreaming-of-white-supremacist-violence.

16. *United States of America v. Alan Hostetter, Russell Taylor, Erik Scott Warner, Felipe Antonio Martinez, Derek Kinnison, and Ronald Mele*, 21-cr-392 (RCL) United States District Court for the District of Columbia, January 8, 2021.

17. Anti-Defamation League, "Three Percenters," July 13, 2020, accessed January 19, 2023, https://www.adl.org/resources/backgrounder/three-percenters.

18. Department of Justice, "Cleveland Man Found Guilty in Plot to Ambush and Kidnap Law Enforcement Officers," Justice.gov, May 7, 2021, accessed January 19, 2023. https://justice.gov/usao-ndoh/pr/cleveland-man-found-guilty-plot-ambush-and-kidnap-law-enforcement-officers.

19. Christy Jankowski, "White Rabbit Militia Leader Sentenced for Domestic Terrorism," *Nexstar Media Wire*, July 13, 2022, http://ktla.com/news/nexstar-media-wire/white-rabbit-militia-leader-sentenced-for-domestic-terrorism/.

20. *See supra* note 16. (*United States of America v. Alan Hostetter, Russell Taylor, Erik Scott Warner, Felipe Antonio Martinez, Derek Kinnison, and Ronald Mele*).

Five: The Big Lies

1. National Consortium for the Study of Terrorism and Responses to Terrorism, "Capitol Insurrection Network Map," accessed February 24, 2023. https://www.start.umd.edu/data-tools/capitol-insurrection-network-map

2. Media Defence, "Module 8: 'False News,' Misinformation and Propaganda," accessed December 19, 2022, https://www.mediadefence.org/ereader/publications/introductory-modules-on-digital-rights-and-freedom-of-expression-online.

3. Terrance Smith, "Trump Has Longstanding History of Calling

Elections 'Rigged' If He Doesn't Like the Results," *ABC News.* November 11, 2020, https://abcnews.go.com/Politics/trump-long-standing-history-calling-elections-rigged-doesnt-results/story?id =74126926

4. Kim Mills, Interview with Dr. Karen Douglas, *Speaking of Psychology,* (podcast), January 2021, https://www.apa.org/news/podcasts/speaking-of-psychology/conspiracy-theories.

5. Pew Research Center, "An Examination of the 2016 Electorate, Based on Validated Voters," August 10, 2018, accessed November 22, 2022, https://www.pewresearch.org/politics/2018/08/09/an-examination-of-the-2016-electorate-based-on-validated-voters/2-12-2.

6. Kim Mills, "Speaking of Psychology: Why People Believe in Conspiracy Theories," *Speaking of Psychology,* Karen Douglas, American Psychological Association, (podcast), January 2021, https://www.apa.org/news/podcasts/speaking-of-psychology/conspiracy-theories.

7. *See supra* note 3 (Smith).

8. Alex Marshall, "Marina Abramovic Just Wants Conspiracy Theorists to Let Her Be," *New York Times,* April 21, 2020, https://www.nytimes.com/2020/04/21/arts/design/marina-abramovic-satanist-conspiracy-theory.html.

9. David Kushner, "4chan's Overlord Christopher Poole Reveals Why He Walked Away," *Rolling Stone,* March 13, 2015, https://www.rollingstone.com/culture/culture-features/4chans-overlord-christopher-poole-reveals-why-he-walked-away-93894.

10. *United States of America v. John Edgar Rust,* 1:17-MJ-56 United States District Court for the Eastern District of Virginia, October 3, 2017.

11. David D. Kirkpatrick, "Who Is Behind QAnon? Linguistic Detectives Find Fingerprints," *New York Times,* February 19, 2022, https://www.nytimes.com/2022/02/19/technology/qanon-messages-authors.html.

12. AP News, "Man Pleads Guilty to Terrorism after Hoover Dam Barricade," *AP News,* https://apnews.com/article/4a977b1627374e 541d5173d4a3d6d987.

13. Ali Watkins, "He Wasn't Seeking to Kill a Mob Boss. He Was

Trying to Help Trump, His Lawyer Says," *New York Times*, July 21, 2019, https://www.nytimes.com/2019/07/21/nyregion/gambino-shooting-anthony-comello-frank-cali.html.

14. *See* note 6 (Mills).

15. Paul P. Murphy, "InfoWars' Alex Jones Helped Jumpstart January 6 Rally Organization Efforts," *CNN*, January 31, 2021, www.cnn.com/2021/01/31/politics/alex-jones-rally-organization-efforts.

16. Jan-Willem van Prooijen and Karen M. Douglas, "Conspiracy Theories as Part of History: The Role of Societal Crisis Situations," *Memory Studies* 10, no. 3 (July 2017), https://doi.org/10.1177/1750698017701615.

17. Adrian Furnham and George Horne, "Cover Ups and Conspiracy Theories: Demographics, Work Disenchantment, Equity Sensitivity, and Beliefs in Cover-ups," *Revista de Psicologia del Trabajo y de lasOrganizaciones* 38, no. 1: 19-25.

18. Joseph Uscinski and Joseph M. Parent, *American Conspiracy Theories*, (Oxford: Oxford University Press, 2014).

19. Mark R. Cheathem, "Conspiracy Theories Abounded in 19th-Century American Politics," *Smithsonian Magazine*, April 11, 2019, https://www.smithsonianmag.com/history/conspiracy-theories-abounded-19th-century-american-politics-180971940.

20. Cheathem, "Conspiracy Theories."

21. Cheathem, "Conspiracy Theories."

22. *The Week* Staff, "A Brief History of Conspiracy Theories," *The Week*, January 8, 2015, https://theweek.com/articles/459843/brief-history-conspiracy-theories.

23. Matthew Rosenberg, "A QAnon Supporter Is Headed to Congress," *New York Times*, November 3, 2020, https://www.nytimes.com/2020/11/03/us/politics/qanon-candidates-marjorie-taylor-greene.html.

24. Reuters Fact Check, "Fact Check-Tweet overstates number of children who went missing in the United States in 2020," *Reuters*, December 13, 2021, https://www.reuters.com/article/factcheck-us-missing/fact-check-tweet overstates-number-of-children-who-went-missing-in-the-united-states-in-2020-idUSL1N2SY199.

Six: What Should Have Happened Next

1. Julie Farnam, "IICDLeads Email Box," (email), January 5, 2021.

2. E.H., "Abuse of Power, Violations of USCP Regulations, and Retaliation," (email), October 13, 2021.

3. US House of Representatives Select Committee to Investigate the January 6th Attack on the United States Capitol, *Final Report of the Select Committee*, 117th Cong., 2022.

4. Mike Spies and Jake Pearson, "Text Messages Show Top Trump Campaign Fundraiser's Key Role Planning the Rally That Preceded the Siege," *ProPublica,* January 30, 2021, https://www.propublica.org/article/trump-campaign-fundraiser-ellipse-rally.

5. Cynthia Chafian, "Permit Application for January 5-7," (email), December 28, 2020.

6. Cynthia Chafian, "Re: January 5–7, 2021," (email), December 26, 2020.

7. Redacted Name, text message, December 14, 2022.

8. Confidential Source, interview by Julie Farnam, April 7, 2022.

9. Confidential Source, April 7, 2022.

10. Charles Anthony Flynn, interview by Select Committee to Investigate the January 6 Attack on the Capitol, October 28, 2021.

11. US House of Representatives Committee on Appropriations, Appropriators Take Action to Understand Capitol Security Failures, 117th Cong., 2021.

12. Intelligence and Interagency Coordination Division, "January 6, 2021 Joint Session of Congress Demonstrations," January 3, 2021, Washington, DC: United States Capitol Police.

13. Steven A. Sund, *Courage Under Fire* (Ashland, OR: Blackstone Publishing, 2022).

14. Sund, *Courage Under Fire.*

15. Sund, *Courage Under Fire.*

16. Sund, *Courage Under Fire,* 321.

Seven: January 6, 2021

1. Exodus 10:6.

2. Julie Farnam, "Protest Crowd Estimates and Live Feed," (email), January 6, 2021.

3. Julie Farnam, "Metro Ridership," (email), January 6, 2021.

4. Sergeant in the Dignitary Protection Division in discussion with the author, January 2023.

5. *See* note 3, Chapter Six, Select Committee.

6. Eddie Burkhalter, "Alabama Man Pleads Guilty to Firearms Offenses in Connection with Jan. 6," *Fox54*, November 12, 2021, https://www.rocketcitynow.com/article/news/local/alabama-man-pleads-guilty-firearms-offenses-jan-6-capitol/525-0646413d-09f3-403a-9ffd-a2a35e4017e1.

7. Federal Bureau of Investigation, "FBI Washington Field Office Releases Video and Additional Information Regarding the Pipe Bomb Investigation," FBI Press Release, September 8, 2021, https://www.fbi.gov/contact-us/field-offices/washingtondc/news/press-releases/fbi-washington-field-office-releases-video-and-additional-information-regarding-the-pipe-bomb-investigation-090821, accessed July 10, 2023.

8. US Senate Committee on Homeland Security and Governmental Affairs and Committee on Rules and Administration, Report Examining the US Capitol Attack, 117th Congress, 2021.

9. US Senate Examining the US Capitol Attack.

10. Joseph M. Hanneman, "Ashli Babbitt Pleaded With Police to Call for Backup Moments Before She Was Shot and Killed," *The Epoch Times*, January 18, 2022, https://www.theepochtimes.com/ashli-babbitt-dramatically-confronted-police-for-not-stopping-rioters_4220583.html.

11. Connor Sheets, "The Radicalization of Kevin Greeson," *ProPublica*, January 15, 2021, https://www.propublica.org/article/the-radicalization-of-kevin-greeson.

12. Peter Hermann and Steve Thompson, "D.C. Medical Examiner Releases Cause of Death for Four People Who Died During Capitol Riot," *Washington Post*, April 7, 2021, https://www.washingtonpost.com/local/public-safety/trump-riot-death-medical-exainer/2021/04/07/53806608-97cf-11eb-a6d0-13d207aadb78_story.html.

13. Peter Hermann and Steve Thompson, "D.C. Medical Examiner.".

14. Ayman M. Mohyeldin and Preeti Varathan, "Rosanne Boyland Was Outside the U.S. Capitol Last January 6. How—and Why—Did She Die?" *Vanity Fair,* January 5, 2022. https://www.vanityfair.com/news/2022/01/capitol-insurrection-rosanne-boyland-how-and-why-did-she-die.

15. Mohyeldin and Varathan, "Rosanne Boyland Was Outside the U.S. Capitol."

16. *See* note 11, Chapter Six (US House of Representatives Committee on Appropriations).

17. Yoganada Pittman in discussion with author, September 2021.

18. Muriel Bowser interview by Select Committee to Investigate the January 6th Attack on the Capitol, January 12, 2022.

19. Robert J. Contee III interview by Select Committee to Investigate the January 6th Attack on the United States Capitol. January 11, 2022.

20. Government Accountability Office, "Capitol Attack: The Capitol Police Need Clearer Emergency Procedures and a Comprehensive Security Risk Assessment Process," GAO-22-105001, accessed February 23, 2023, https://www.gao.gov/assets/gao-22-105001.pdf.

21. Yogananda Pittman interview by Select Committee to Investigate the January 6th Attack on the United States Capitol, January 13, 2022.

Eight: Seditious Conspiracies

1. Dayook Wong, "The Psychology of Mob Mentality," *Psychology Today,* January 24, 2021, https://www.psychologytoday.com/us/blog/facing-trauma-together/202101/the-psychology-mob-mentality.

2. Title 18 U.S.C. § 2384 (1940).

3. James B. Kelleher and Rachelle Damico, "Hutaree Militia Walk From Jail After Charges Dismissed," *Reuters,* March 29, 2012, https://www.reuters.com/article/us-usa-crime-militia/hutaree-militia-walk-from-jailaftercharges-dismissed-idUSBRE-82S1EX20120329.

4. Alanna Durkin Richer and Lindsay Whitehurst, "EXPLAINER: Rare Sedition Charge at Center of Jan. 6 Trial," *Washington Post,* September 28, 2022, https://apnews.com/article/what-does-sedition-charge-mean-3aa820dda5f501dd874c4dd6d60ca1ce.

5. Henry Tarrio, interview by Select Committee to Investigate the January 6th Attack on the United States Capitol, February 4, 2022.

6. *See* note 12, Chapter Four (Rhodes III).

7. Aram Roston, "FBI Probes Pre-Capitol Riot Meeting of Far-Right Groups." *Reuters*, February 8, 2022, https://www.reuters.com/world/us/exclusive-fbi-probes-pre-capitol-riot-meeting-far-right-groups-2022-02-08/.

8. *See* note 4 (Richer and Whitehurst).

9. Spencer S. Hsu, 2022. "Video Released of Garage Meeting of Proud Boys, Oath Keepers Leaders," *Washington Post*, May 24 : https://www.washingtonpost.com/dc-md-va/2022/05/24/tarrio-rhodes-video/.

10. Hsu, "Video Released."

11. *See* note 5 (Tarrio).

12. *See* note 7 (Roston).

13. *United States of America v. Elmer Stewart Rhodes III et al.,* 2022. 21-cr-15 (APM) Superseding Indictment United States District Court for the District of Columbia, June 22, 2022.

14. *See* note 21, Chapter Seven (Select Committee).

15. Marshall Cohen, "Oath Keepers Likely Stashed Weapons at a Comfort Inn Prior to Capitol Riot, Prosecutors Say," *CNN*, April 14, 2021, https://www.cnn.com/2021/04/13/politics/oath-keepers-comfort-inn/index.html.

16. *See* note 13 (*United States of America v. Elmer Stewart Rhodes III et al.*).

17. Spencer S. Hsu, Rachel Weiner, and Tom Jackman, "U.S.: Oath Keepers, Rhodes Attacked 'Bedrock of Democracy' on Jan. 6," *Washington Post*, October 3, 2022, https://www.washingtonpost.com/dc-md-va/2022/10/03/oath-keepers-trial-openings-rhodes.

18. Kyle Cheney, "Prosecutors Detail Oath Keepers' Mounting Frustration with Trump as Jan. 6 Approached," *Politico*, October 20, 2022, https://www.politico.com/news/2022/10/20/oath-keepers-trump-jan-6-00062779.

19. *See* note 13 (*United States of America v. Elmer Stewart Rhodes III et al.*).

20. Carter Walker, "Seattle Proud Boy Reveals He Was in Council Alleged to Have Planned Jan. 6 Insurrection," *Seattle Times*, July 7, 2022, https://www.seattletimes.com/seattle-news/times-watchdog/seattle-proud-boy-reveals-he-was-in-chapter-alleged-to-have-planned-jan-6-insurrection.

21. Proud Boys., "1776 Returns," December 2020.

Nine: The Toll Taken

1. Bart Jansen, "Missed Warnings of Capitol Riot Echo Intelligence Lapses Before Shootings, 9/11," *USA Today*, June 15, 2021, https://www.usatoday.com/story/news/politics/elections/2021/06/15/capitol-riot-intelligence-failures/7658727002/?gnt-cfr=1.

2. James B. Abbott, "Threats to Bring Guns Into DC," (email), December 22, 2020.

3. *See* note 21, Chapter Seven (Select Committee).

4. Julie Farnam, "Social Media Threat," (email), December 22, 2020.

5. Alexandra Ferraro, "FYSA OSINT Threat Report: User in Far-Right Chat Group Threatens to 'Shoot and Kill' Counter-Protesters," (email), December 23, 2020.

6. Guillermo Rivera, "January 6th Website," (email), December 23, 2020.

7. John K. Donohue, "Armed and Ready, Mr. President," (email), December 27, 2020.

8. AD-Keith Williams, "Fwd:," (email), December 30, 2020.

9. John K. Donohue, "Re:," (email), January 1, 2021.

10. Julie Farnam, "MPD MMS Text Tip," (email), January 1, 2021.

11. Julie Farnam, "*Washington Post* Article," (email), January 3, 2021.

12. John K. Donohue, "Call into cic ref carrying weapons," (email), January 4, 2021.

13. Jonathan Hooks, "Parler Posts," (email), January 4, 2021.

14. Jeanita Mitchell, "Subject claiming to come to DC with Weapons," (email), January 4, 2021.

15. Donell Harvin, "Raw Reporting DC Threat," (email), January 5, 2021.

16. Steven A. Sund, *Courage Under Fire* (Ashland, OR: Blackstone Publishing, 2022), 241.

17. FBI Situational Information Report, https://www.justsecurity.org/wp-content/uploads/2021/12/january-6-clearinghouse-norfolk-report-january-5-2021.pdf

18. FBI Situation Information Report.

19. Jack Date, "Former Capitol Police Chief Steven Sund Says Entire Intelligence Community Missed Signs of Riot," *ABC News*, February 6, 2021. https://abcnews.go.com/Politics/capitol-police-chief-steven-sund-entire-intelligence-community/story?id=75729882.

20. Steven Sund, letter to Nancy Pelosi, Washington, DC, February 1, 2021.

21. Julie Farnam, "Bulletin 21.5: Support Services Available to USCP Employees," (email), January 10, 2021.

22. K.B., "SCIF Coverage," (email), January 6, 2021.

23. K.B., "Joint Sessions Folder," (email), January 7, 2021.

24. K.B., "Flagging Threat: Bomb DC," (email), January 11, 2021.

25. William Vaillancourt, "DHS Whistleblower: Trump Team Wanted Us to Lie About Russia, the Border, and White Supremacy," *Rolling Stone*, September 26, 2021. https://www.rollingstone.com/politics/politics-news/brian-murphy-whistleblower-trump-border-russia-racism-1232427/.

Ten: High Stakes

1. Kimberly Schneider, "Sunday Morning," (email), January 3, 2021.

2. US House of Representatives GOP January 6th Shadow Committee, Report of Investigation: Security Failures at the United States Capitol on January 6, 2021, 117th Cong., 2022.

3. S.R., "21-A-0178 Sen. Ernst, IA Nov 3.doc," (email), October 30, 2020.

4. S.R., "Saturday Coverage," (email), November 5, 2020.

5. S.R., "District Event Spreadsheet," (email), November 7, 2020.

6. S.R., "Election Results," (email), November 7, 2020.

7. S.R., "Routine Social Media Searches," (email), November 9, 2020.

8. K.R., "IICD Training," (email), March 10, 2021.

9. K.R., "Updates," (email), November 9, 2020.

10. K.R., "Threats," (email), December 22, 2020.

11. *See* note 7 ("Routine Social Media Searches").

12. Whitney Wild and Zachary Cohen, "Exclusive: Inside the Capitol Police Intelligence Unit Overhaul that Caused Confusion Ahead of January 6," CNN, November 5, 2021, https://www.cnn.com/2021/11/05/politics/jan-6-capitol-police-intelligence-unit-overhaul/index.html.

13. *See* note 2 (US House of Representatives GOP January 6th Shadow Committee).

14. D.M. ,"Urgent Request," Whitney Wild Cohen and Zachary. "Exclusive: Inside the Capitol Police intelligence unit overhaul that caused confusion ahead of January, May 4, 2021.

15. Karen Miller in discussion with author, November 2021.

16. Revelations 6:1-3.

17. Peter Hermann, Matt Zapotosky, Michelle Boorstein and Jessica Contrera, "One Officer Dead After Car Rams Capitol Barricade; Suspect Fatally Shot by Police, Officials Say," *Washington Post*, April 2, 2021, https://www.washingtonpost.com/local/public-safety/capitol-lockdown-police-officers-injured-barricade-rammed/2021/04/02/1e1820aa-93d8-11eb-a74e-1f4cf89fd948_story.html.

18. Julie Farnam, (email), June 3, 2021.

19. Kimberly A. Schneider, (email), June 3, 2021.

Eleven: Regrouped and Reinvigorated

1. National Intelligence Council, "Foreign Threats to the 2020 US Federal Elections," accessed February 23, 2023. https://www.dni.gov/files/ODNI/documents/assessments/ICA-declass-16MAR21.pdf.

2. The Armed Conflict Location & Event Data Project 2022, "From the Capitol Riot to the Midterms: Shifts in American Far-Right Mobilization Between 2021 and 2022," accessed February 24, 2023. https://acleddata.com/2022/12/06/from-the-capitol-riot-to-the-midterms-shifts-in-american-far-right-mobilization-between-2021-and-2022/

3. The Armed Conflict Location & Event Data Project 2022.

4. The Armed Conflict Location & Event Data Project. 2022.

5. Department of Justice, "2021 Hate Crime Statistics," December 13, 2021, accessed January 21, 2023, https://www.justice.gov/hatecrimes/hate-crime-statistics.

6. Southern Poverty Law Center, "Hate Map By State," accessed July 15, 2023, https://www.splcenter.org/20220309/year-hate-extremism-report-2021.

7. Tess Owen, "The Proud Boys Changed Tactics After Jan. 6. We Tracked Their Activity," *Vice News*, January 5, 2022, www.vice.com/en/article/z3n338/what-the-proud-boys-did-after-jan-6.

8. Michael Kunzelman Richer and Alanna Durkin, "Capitol Insurrection Aftermath Roils Far-Right Extremist Groups," *AP News*, June 2, 2021. https://pbs.org/newshour/nation/capitol-insurrection-aftermath-roils-far-right-extremist-groups.

9. Aram Roston, "Exclusive: Proud Boys Leader Was 'Prolific' Informer for Law Enforcement," *Reuters*, January 27, 2021, https://reuters.com/article/us-usa-proudboys-leader-exclusive/exclusive-proud-boys-leader-was-prolific-informer-for-law-enforcement-idUSKBN29W1PE.

10. Clio Chang, "The Unlikely Rise of an Alt-Right Hero," *New Republic*, March 31, 2017, https://newrepublic.com/article/141766/unlikely-rise-alt-right-hero.

11. Ewan Palmer, "Proud Boys Infighting Sees Leading Member Form Breakaway Group to Fight 'White Genocide'," *Newsweek*, November 11. 2020. https://www.newsweek.com/proud-boys-based-stickman-enrique-tarrio-goys-1546597

12. Kelly Weill, "Former Proud Boy Leader 'Based Stickman' Arrested for Attacking Health Care Workers," *The Daily Beast*, January 12, 2022, https://www.thedailybeast.com/former-proud-boys-leader-kyle-based-stickman-chapman-arrested-for-attacking-health-care-workers-in-idaho.

13. Alex Brizee, "White Nationalist Sentenced to 3 Months in Jail After Battering Health Care Worker," *Spokesman-Review*, December 27, 2022, https://www.spokesman.com/stories/2022/dec/27/white-nationalist-sentenced-to-3-months-in-jail-af.

14. Enrique Tarrio, interview by United States Capitol Police Special Agent, January 13, 2022.

15. Will Sommer, "Gavin McInnes Attempts to Quash Proud Boys' Post-Jan. 6 'Civil War'," *The Daily Beast*, October 9, 2022, https://thedailybeast.com/gavin-mcinnes-attempts-to-quash-proud-boys-post-jan-6-civil-war?ref=scroll.

16. Will Carless and Ella Lee, "Two Years Since the Jan. 6 Insurrection, Extremist Groups Are Fragmented, But Live On," *USA Today*, January 6, 2023, https://www.usatoday.com/story/news/nation/2023/01/06/proud-boys-oath-keepers-qanon-two-years-after-jan-6/10998158002/.

17. WhiteLivesMatterOfficial, "Illinois North, West Central and Missouri," Gab, January 21, 2023, https://gab.com/WhiteLivesMatterOfficial/posts/109723833439640072.

18. Cole's Dad Don (@Don1975), "Reposted by Esoteric Doge," Gab, January 19, 2023, https://gab.com/Don1975/posts/109733416238680130.

19. Anti-Defamation League, "White Supremacist Propaganda Soars to All-Time High in 2022," March 8, 2023, accessed July 15, 2023, https://www.adl.org/resources/report/white-supremacist-propaganda-soars-all-time-high-2022.

20. Anti-Defamataion League, "White Supremacist Propaganda."

21. Mack Lamoureux and David Gilbert, "Q Is Dead, Long Live QAnon," *Vice News*, November 15, 2022, https://www.vice.com/en/article/wxnkzq/qanon-q-drop-midterms.

22. Shayan Sardarizadeh, "Why are QAnon Believers Obsessed with 4 March?" *BBC News*, March 4, 2021, https://www.bbc.com/news/blogs-trending-56260345.

23. Public Religion Research Institute, "The Persistence of QAnon in the Post-Trump Era," accessed February 23, 2023, https://www.prri.org/wp-content/uploads/2022/02/PRRI-Feb-2022-Qanon-final.pdf.

24. Zöe Richard, "Republicans Lash Out at Justice Department After FBI Searches Trump's Mar-a-Lago Home," *NBC News*, August 8, 2022, https://www.nbcnews.com/politics/donald-trump/republicans-lash-justice-department-fbi-searches-trumps-mar-lago-home-rcna42139.

25. Robert Draper, *Weapons of Mass Delusion: When the Republican Party Lost Its Mind* (New York: Penguin Press, 2022).

26. Public Religion Research Institute Staff, "A Christian Nation? Understanding the Threat of Christian Nationalism to American Democracy and Culture," February 8, 2023, accessed July 15, 2023, https://www.prri.org/research/a-christian-nation-understanding-the-threat-of-christian-nationalism-to-american-democracy-and-culture/.

27. Aja Romano, "The Right's Moral Panic Over 'Grooming' Invokes Age-Old Homophobia," *Vox*, April 21, 2022, https://www.vox.com/culture/23025505/leftist-groomers-homophobia-satanic-panic-explained.

28. Anti-Defamation League, "QAnon's Antisemitism and What Comes Next," September 17, 2021, accessed January 22, 2023, https://www.adl.org/resources/report/qanons-antisemitism-and-what-comes-next.

29. Erika D. Smith and Anita Chabria, "Column: White Supremacy Comes in All Colors. 2023 Will Make This Impossible to Ignore," *Los Angeles Times*, January 1, 2023, https://www.latimes.com/california/story/2023-01-01/new-year-2023-white-supremacy-extremism-antisemitism-hate-comes-all-colors.

30. House of Wagner (@HausWagner), "BEFORE YOUTUBE BEFORE ONLYFANS BEFORE TIKTOK BEFORE CNN," *Gab*, January 15, 2023, https://gab.com/HausWagner/posts/109696420032541899.

31. Erika D. Smith and Anita Chabria, "Column: White Supremacy Comes in All Colors."

32. *See* note 1, Chapter Eleven (National Intelligence Council).

33. Josh Margolin and Teddy Grant, "Threats Against the LGBTQIA+ Community Intensifying: Department of Homeland Security," *ABC News*, May 15, 2023, https://abcnews.go.com/US/threats-lgbtqia-community-intensifying-department-homeland-security/story?id=99338137.

34. Kiara Alfonseca, "Threats and Violence: LGBTQ Community Faces Renewed Political Battles During Pride Month," *ABC News*,

June 21, 2023, https://abcnews.go.com/US/threats-violence-lgbtq-community-faces-renewed-political-battles/story?id=85409645.

35. Meg Woolhouse Phillip Martin, "Neo-Nazi Leader Arrested in Boston After Protesting LGBTQ Event," *WGBH*, July 23, 2022, https://www.wgbh.org/news/local-news/2022/07/23/neo-nazi-leader-arrested-in-boston-after-protesting-lgbtq-event.

36. NSC-131 New England (@NewEngland131), "NSC 131 Activists Protested Outside of a Drag Queen Story Hour in Concord, New Hampshire," Gab, June 22, 2023, https://gab.com/NewEngland131/posts/110589977429074563.

37. WION Web Team, "Tesla CEO Elon Musk Believes This Is the 'Biggest Threat' to Modern Civilisation," *WION News*, December 22, 2021, https://www.wionews.com/world/tesla-ceo-elon-musk-believes-this-is-the-biggest-threat-to-modern-civilisation-438996.

38. Southern Poverty Law Center, "Exposing Extremism in Elections," accessed February 8, 2023, https://www.splcactionfund.org/projects/exposing-extremism-elections.

39. National Consortium for the Study of Terrorism and Responses to Terrorism, "Extremism in the Ranks and After," accessed August 9, 2023, https://www.start.umd.edu/sites/default/files/publications/local_attachments/Extremism%20In%20the%20Ranks%20and%20After%20-%20Research%20Brief%20-%20April%202023%20Final.pdf.

40. Department of Defense, *Handling Protest, Extremist, and Criminal Gang Activities Among Members of the Armed Forces,* DOD Instruction 1325.06. Arlington, VA: Department of Defense, 2021, https://www.esd.whs.mil/Portals/54/Documents/DD/issuances/dodi/132506p.PDF.

41. Hanna Krueger, "'The Single Biggest Threat to the Security of the Country': Extremism in the Military Is Alarming Experts," *Boston Globe*, July 15, 2023, https://www.bostonglobe.com/2023/07/15/nation/extremism-in-military-big-security-threat/?event=event12.

Twelve: Investigations and Testimony

1. United States Capitol Police Office of Inspector General, *Evaluation of the United States Capitol Police Division of Intelligence*

and Information Analysis, OIG-2016-04, (Washington, DC, March 2016).

2. United States Capitol Police Office of Inspector General, *Review of the Events Surrounding the January 6, 2021, Takeover of the U.S. Capitol. Flash Report: Operational Planning and Intelligence,* OIG-2021-I-0003-A, (Washington, DC, 2021).

3. *See* note 9, Chapter Seven (US Senate Examining the US Capitol Attack).

4. *See* note 11, Chapter Six (US House of Representatives Committee on Appropriations).

5. US Senate Committee on Homeland Security and Governmental Affairs, Joint Full Committee Hearing: Examining the January 6 Attack on the US Capitol, 117th Cong., 2021.

6. U.S. Senate Committee on Homeland Security.

7. Briefing on the January 6, 2021 Attack on the Capitol, Before the House Subcommittee on the Legislative Branch, 117th Congress, February 25, 2021, (testimony of Yogananda Pittman).

8. United States Capitol Police, *United States Capitol Police Timeline of Events for January 6, 2021 Attack,* Washington, DC: GPO, 2021.

9. *See* note 9, Chapter Seven (US Senate Examining the US Capitol Attack).

10. US Senate Examining the US Capitol Attack).

11. *See* note 14, Chapter Ten, (Capitol Police Intelligence Assessment).

12. Chris Van Cleave and Michael Kaplan, "Capitol Police Intelligence Official Says She Sounded Alarm about Potential Violence Days Before January 6 Riot," *CBS News,* January 5, 2022, https://www.cbsnews.com/news/capitol-police-intelligence-official-julie-farnam-january-6-riot/.

13. *See* note 13, Chapter Six (Sund).

14. Tim Barber, conversation with Daniel Lippman, (phone call), January 22, 2021.

15. Betsy Woodruff Swan and Daniel Lippman, "Capitol Police Examines Backgrounds, Social Media Feeds of Some Who Meet with Lawmakers., *Politico,* January 24, 2021, https://www.politico.com/news/2022/01/24/capitol-police-social-media-00000948.

16. United States Capitol Police Office of Inspector General,

Review of Intelligence and Interagency Coordination Division Processes and Procedures Surrounding the Protection of Member Events, OIG-2022-I-0004, (Washington, DC, 2022).

17. *See* note 15 (Woodruff).

18. *See* note 16 (OIG, *Review of Intelligence and Interagency Coordination Division Processes*).

19. *See* note 15 (Woodruff).

20. *See* note 16 (OIG *Review of Intelligence and Interagency Coordination Division Processes*).

21. *See* note 3, Chapter One, (US House of Representatives GOP January 6th Shadow Committee).

22. Jeffrey J. Pickett, "Letter to Nancy Pelosi, Chuck Schumer, Kevin McCarthy, and Mitch McConnell," Washington, DC, September 28, 2021.

23. Jeffrey J. Pickett, "Letter to the Committee on House Administration and the U.S. Senate Committee on Rules & Administration," Washington, DC, November 2021.

24. Jeffrey J. Pickett, "Letter to Nancy Pelosi, et al."

25. Jeffrey J. Pickett, "Letter to Nancy Pelosi, et al."

26. D.M., "FMLA Request-UPDATE," (email), November 16, 2021.

27. Rachael Weiner, Spencer S. Hsu, and Peter Hermann, "U.S.: Proud Boys Leader Learned of Upcoming Arrest from D.C. Police officer," *Washington Post,* February 15, 2023, https://www.washingtonpost.com/dc-md-va/2023/02/15/lamond-tarrio-jan6-trial/.

28. Peter Hermann, "Police Supervisor Chatted Up Patriot Front Poser Who Recorded It All," *Washington Post,* September 3, 2022, https://www.washingtonpost.com/dc-md-va/2022/09/03/patriot-front-dc-police-conversations/.

29. USCP Inspector, "LNOEVENT Distro," (email), March 17, 2022.

30. *See* note 7 (Briefing on the January 6, 2021 Attack on the Capitol).

31. United States Capitol Police, "Draft Responses to GAO Follow-Up Questions (GAO 104793)," Washington, DC, May 18, 2022.

32. Government Accountability Office, *Capitol Attack: The Capitol Police Need Clearer Emergency Procedures and a Comprehensive Security*

Risk Assessment Proces, GAO-22-105001, (Washington, DC, 2022), accessed February 23, 2023, https://www.gao.gov/assets/gao-22-105001.pdf.

Thirteen: Countering Extremism

1. Allison G. Smith, "How Radicalization to Terrorism Occurs in the United States: What Research Sponsored by the National Institute of Justice Tells Us," *National Institute of Justice,* accessed February 23, 2023, https://www.ojp.gov/pdffiles1/nij/250171.pdf.

2. Rosanna E. Guandagno, Adam Lankford, Nicole L. Muscanell, Bradley M. Okdie, and Debra M. McCallum, "Social Influence in the Online Recruitment of Terrorists and Terrorist Sympathizers: Implications for Social Psychology Research," *Revue Internationale de Psychologie Sociale* 23 (January 2010): 25–56.

3. Allison G. Smith, "How Radicalization to Terrorism, etc."

4. P. Rozin, L. Lowery, S. Imada, and J Haidt, *Journal of Personality and Social Psychology* 76, no. 4 (April 1995): 574–86. https://doi.org/10.1037//0022-3514.76.4.574.

5. MacKenzie Ryan, "A White Nationalist Pyramid Scheme: How Patriot Front Recruits Young Member," *The Guardian,* September 2, 2022, https://theguardian.com/us-news/2022/sep/02/patriot-front-recruits-members-young-pyramid-scheme.

6 Allison G. Smith, "How Radicalization to Terrorism, etc."

7. Rosanna E. Guadagno, et al., "Social Influence in the Online Recruitment of Terrorists and Terrorist Sympathizers: Implications for Social Psychology Research," *Revue Internationale de Psychologie Sociale,* vol. 23, no. 1, 2010, pp. 25-56.

8. Anti-Defamation League, "Andrew Anglin: Five Things to Know," April 25, 2018, accessed January 11, 2023, https://www.adl.org/resources/news/andrew-anglin-five-things-know.

9. Allison G. Smith, "How Radicalization to Terrorism, etc."

10. Maria Cramer, "Fear Spreads in Minnesota Town as 'Extremist Group' Moves to Open Church," *New York Times,* January 9, 2021, https://www.nytimes.com/2021/01/09/us/minnesota-asatru-folk-assembly.html.

11. *See* note 4, Chapter Three, (Gendron)

12. Department of Homeland Security, *Pathways to Violence* (Washington, DC: Department of Homeland Security, 2022).

13. Terrorgram, "Path to Sainthood," November 2, 2022.

14. Federal Bureau of Investigation, National Counterterrorism Center, and Department of Homeland Security, "Mobilization Indicators 2021," accessed January 19, 2023, https://www.dni.gov/ index.php/nctc-newsroom/nctc-resources/item/2272-u-s-violent-extremist-mobilization-indicators-2021.

15. Department of Homeland Security, "Center for Prevention Programs and Partnerships," October 14, 2022, accessed January 30, 2023, https://www.dhs.gov/CP3.

16. Department of Homeland Security, "Center for Prevention Programs and Partnerships."

17. Counter Terrorism Policing, "Prevent," accessed January 31, 2023, https://www.counterterrorism.police.uk/what-we-do/prevent/.

18. European Commission Migration and Home Affairs, "EXIT-Deutschland," May 26, 2021, accessed January 30, 2023, https://home-affairs.ec.europa.eu/networks/radicalisation-awareness-network-ran/collection-inspiring-practices/ran-practices/exit-deutschland_en.

19. Ángel Gómez, Mercedes Martínez, Francois Alexi Martel, Lucía López-Rodríguez, Alexandra Vázquez, Juana Chinchilla, Borja Paredes, Mal Hettiarachchi, Nafees Hamid, and William B. Swann, "Why People Enter and Embrace Violent Groups," *Frontiers in Psychology* 11 (2021): https://doi.org/10.3389/fpsyg.2020.614657.

20. Federal Bureau of Investigation, "What We Investigate," accessed January 31, 2023.,https://www.fbi.gov/investigate/terrorism.

21. Heather J. Williams, Luke J. Matthews, Pauline Moore, Matthew A. DeNardo, James V. Marrone, Brian A. Jackson, William Marcellino, and Todd C. Helmus, "A Dangerous Web: Mapping Racially and Ethnically Motivated Violent Extremism," RAND Corporation, Santa Monica, CA: 2022. https://www.rand.org/pubs/research_briefs/RBA1841-1.html.

22. Digital Citizens Alliance, "The Domestic Extremist Next Door," accessed February 23, 2023, https://www.digitalcitizensalliance.org/

clientuploads/directory/Reports/DCA_The_Domestic_Extremist_
Next_Door.pdf.

23. Denise Lavoie, "Jury Awards $26M in Damages for Unite
the Right Violence," *Associated Press*, November 23, 2021, https://
apnews.com/article/violence-lawsuits-race-and-ethnicity-charlottes-
ville-01d9437ec28ed71b4bae293d7e0d815d.

24. Chris Van Buskirk, "Christopher Hood, Neo-Nazi Leader,
Charged with Violating New Hampshire Civil Rights Act," *MassLive*,
January 17, 2023, https://www.masslive.com/police-fire/2023/01/
christopher-hood-neo-nazi-leader-charged-with-violating-new-
hampshire-civil-rights-act.html.

Fourteen: What Comes Next

1. Oversight of the Federal Bureau of Investigation: the January 6
Insurrection, Domestic Terrorism, and Other Threats, 117th Cong.
"Testimony of Christopher Wray before the Senate Committee on
the Judiciary," March 2, 2021.

2. The Armed Conflict Location & Event Data Project 2022, "From
the Capitol Riot to the Midterms: Shifts in American Far-Right
Mobilization Between 2021 and 2022," ACLED, accessed February
24, 2023, https://acleddata.com/2022/12/06/from-the-capitol-ri-
ot-to-the-midterms-shifts-in-american-far-right-mobilization-be-
tween-2021-and-2022.

3. Steven Simon and Jonathan Stevenson, "The Threat of Civil
Breakdown is Real," *Politico*, April 21, 2023, https://www.polit-
ico.com/news/magazine/2023/04/21/political-violence-2024-
magazine-00093028

4. National Security Council, "National Strategy for Countering
Domestic Terrorism," accessed February 23, 2023, https://www.
whitehouse.gov/wp-content/uploads/2021/06/National-Strategy-
for-Countering-Domestic-Terrorism.pdf.

5. Ross W. Bellaby, *The Ethics of Intelligence: A New Framework.*
(Oxfordshire, UK: Routledge, 2014).

6. Kevin Macnish, "Digital Sleeper Cells and the Ethics of Risk
Management," in *National Security Intelligence and Ethics*, ed. Seamus

Miller, Milton Reagan, and Patrick F. Walsh, (Oxfordshire, UK: Routledge, 2022), 158–74.

7. Catherine Doxsee, Seth G. Jones, Jared Thompson, Kateryna Halstead, and Grace Hwang, "Pushed to Extremes: Domestic Terrorism Amid Polarization and Protest," May 17, 2022, Center for Strategic & International Studies, accessed January 27, 2023, https://www.csis.org/analysis/pushed-extremes-domestic-terrorism-amid-polarization-and-protest.

8. *See* note 4 (National Security Council).

9. Southern Poverty Law Center, "The Base," accessed January 27, 2023. www.splcenter.org/fighting-hate/extremist-files/group/base.

10. Anti-Defamation League, "Soliders of Odin USA," accessed January 25, 2023, https://www.adl.org/sites/default/files/documents/assets/pdf/combating-hate/Soldiers-of-Odin-USA-Report-web.pdf.

11. Matthew Kriner and Jon Lewis, "Pride & Prejudice: The Violent Evolution of the Proud Boys," *Combating Terrorism Center* 14, no. 6, July/August 2021, https://doi.org/https://ctc.westpoint.edu/pride-prejudice-the-violent-evolution-of-the-proud-boys/.

12. Phil Helsel, "Two Men Allegedly Linked to 'Boogaloo' Accused of Offering to Work with Hamas," *NBC News*, September 5, 2020, https://www.nbcnews.com/news/us-news/two-men-allegedly-linked-boogaloo-accused-offering-work-hamas-n1239400.

13. Homeland Security Act of 2002, § 101(a)(1) (2002).

14. Aaron Mehta, "DHS Report in 2009 Warned of 'Lone Wolf' Attacks," *The Center for Public Integrity*, January 10, 2011. https://publicintegrity.org/national-security/dhs-report-in-2009-warned-of-lone-wolf-attacks/.

15. Christian Beckner, "Reassessing Homeland Security Intelligence," *Center for a New American Security*, May 25, 2021, https://www.cnas.org/publications/reports/reassessing-homeland-security-intelligence.

16. Shane Harris, "DHS Compiled 'Intelligence Reports' on Journalists Who Published Leaked Documents," *Washington Post*, July 30, 2020, https://www.washingtonpost.com/national-security/dhs-compiled-intelligence-reports-on-journalists-who-published-leaked-documents/2020/07/30/5be5ec9e-d25b-11ea-9038-

af089b63ac21_story.html.

17. Brian Murphy, "Whistleblower Reprisal Complaint," September 8, 2020., https://int.nyt.com/data/documenttools/homeland-security-whistleblower/0819ec9ee29306a5/full.pdf.

18. Brian Murphy, "Whistleblower Reprisal."

19. Brian Murphy, "Whistleblower Reprisal."

20. *See* note 14 (Mehta).

21. Mark MacCarthy, "A Consumer Protection Approach to Platform Content Moderation," *SSRN Electronic Journal*, 2019, https://doi.org/10.2139/ssrn.3408459.

22. Communications Decency Act, U.S.C. 47 § 230 (1996)

23. Knight First Amendment Institute at Columbia University, "Twitter v. Taamneh in the Supreme Court: What's at Stake," December 12, 2022, accessed February 15, 2023, https://knightcolumbia.org/blog/twitter-v-taamneh-in-the-supreme-court-whats-at-stake.

24. Exec. Order. No. 13925, 85 Fed. Reg. 34079 (May 28, 2020), https://www.federalregister.gov/documents/2020/06/02/2020-12030/preventing-online-censorship.

25. Kelly Rissman, "Did Rep. George Santos Flash the White Power Symbol in the House Chamber?" *Vanity Fair*, January 8, 2023, https://www.vanityfair.com/news/2023/01/did-rep-george-santos-flash-the-white-power-symbol-in-the-house-chamber.

26. Aaron Blake, "How the Ilhan Omar Committee Vote Compares to Marjorie Taylor Greene's," *Washington Post*, January 27, 2023, https://www.washingtonpost.com/politics/2023/01/27/greene-omar-committee-votes.

27. Trip Gabriel, "A Website for a GOP House Candidate Flings a Racist Attack at a Journalist," *New York Times*, October 23, 2020, https://www.nytimes.com/2020/10/23/us/elections/a-website-for-a-gop-house-candidate-flings-a-racist-attack-at-a-journalist.html.

28. Jonathan Weisman and Annie Karni, "GOP Leaders Condemn Lawmakers' Appearance at White Nationalist Conference," *New York Times*, February 28, 2022, https://www.nytimes.com/2022/02/28/us/politics/republicans-extremism-marjorie-taylor-greene.html.

29. Brian Slodysko, "GOP's Links to Extremism Surface in Congressional Primary," *AP News*, July 27, 2022, https://apnews.

com/article/2022-midterm-elections-donald-trump-campaigns-race-and-ethnicity-be616cae0967ca6ee9c78ac1efee8e31.

30. Susan Milligan, "From Embrace to 'Replace'," *U.S. News and World Report*, May 20, 2022. https://www.usnews.com/news/the-report/articles/2022-05-20/the-republican-embrace-of-the-great-replacement-theory.

31. Graeme Massie, "Lauren Boebert Shares QAnon Conspiracy Claiming Democratic Arrests and Resignations," *The Independent*, March 19, 2021, https://www.independent.co.uk/news/world/americas/us-politics/boebert-gop-qanon-congress-democrats-b1819868.html.

32. Bob Good, "Congressman Bob Good," September 29, 2022, accessed January 8, 2023, https://good.house.gov/media/press-releases/rep-bob-good-introduces-defending-students-civil-rights-act-2021.

33. Dutin Stockton interview by Select Committee to Investigate the January 6th Attack on the United States Capitol, December 14, 2021.

34. James Phillips, "Combatting Terrorism in the Wake of the Oklahoma City Bombing," *Heritage Foundation*, April 26, 1995, accessed January 24, 2023, https://www.heritage.org/homeland-security/report/combatting-terrorism- the-wake-the-oklahoma-city-bombing.

35. *Domestic Terrorism Prevention Act of 2022*, H.R. 350, 117th Congress. (2022).

36. Retro Report, *Extremism in America: The Oklahoma City Bombing*, 2022, accessed August 20, 2023, https://www.retroreport.org/video/extremism-in-america-the-oklahoma-city-bombing.

37. UNESCO, "Preventing Violent Extremism," accessed January 30, 2023, https://en.unesco.org/preventingviolentextremism.

38. Jarrett Stepman, "DeSantis Deals Blow to Woke Takeover of Education," Heritage Foundation, January 26, 2023, accessed January 29, 2023, https://www.heritage.org/education/commentary/desantis-deals-blow-woke-takeover-education.

39. Kyle Cheney, "Jan. 6 Defendant Who Sprayed Line of Police Sentenced after Tearful Apology," *Politico*, January 1, 2023, www.politico.com/news/2023/02/01/jan-6-defendent-sentenced-0080732.

40. Tom Jackman, "Md. Man Who Sprayed Fire Extinguisher at

Police on Jan. 6 Given 33-Month Prison Term," *Washington Post*, May 23, 2022, https://www.washingtonpost.com/dc-md-va/2022/05/23/miller-sentenced-jan6.

41. Alexander Mallin, "Just Before Jan. 6 Hearing, 3 Capitol Rioters Express Regret, Ask for Mercy," *ABC News*, June 9, 2022, www.abcnews.go.com/politics/jan-hearing-capitol-rioters-express-regret-mercy/story?id=85290390.

42. Alanna Durkin Richer and Michael Kunzelman, "Sorry, Not Sorry: Some 1/6 Rioters Change Tune after Apology," *AP News*, February 3, 2023, https://apnews.com/article/jan6-capitol-riot-participants-change-tune-after-apologies-f0f37e1409da9366d2d3cc3de65502d9.